Two Views
of Waterloo

Two Views of Waterloo

Flying Sketches of the Battle of Waterloo

Newman Smith

Some Particulars of the Battle of Waterloo

C.W.

LEONAUR

Two Views of Waterloo
Flying Sketches of the Battle of Waterloo
by Newman Smith
and
Some Particulars of the Battle of Waterloo
by C. W.

First published under the titles

Flying Sketches of the Battle of Waterloo, &c., &c.
and
Some Particulars of the Battle of Waterloo

Leonaur is an imprint of Oakpast Ltd

ISBN: 978-0-85706-339-7 (hardcover)
ISBN:978-0-85706-340-3 (softcover)

http://www.leonaur.com

Contents

Flying Sketches of the Battle of Waterloo   7

Some Particulars of the Battle of Waterloo   79

Flying Sketches of the Battle of Waterloo

Newman Smith

Contents

Flying Sketch of the Battle of Waterloo 11

Flying Sketch of the Battle of Waterloo

However little it may interest others to know that only a few hours' notice was afforded me, to accept or refuse an invitation to visit Flanders on the 6th of June, 1815, I cannot note down the commencement of my journal without remembering how little I felt disposed at the time to undertake a trip, which I would not afterwards have lost for a thousand pounds; and that (invalid as I was) my ultimate decision to effect it, arose more from the hope of being benefited by a sea voyage, than from any expectation of pleasure in the enjoyment of it. But—

Thus are human calculations incomplete.

On the evening of the 6th of June, I reached Ramsgate, and found Capt. Clarke, with our mutual friend Mr. Meryon, on board their little yacht, the *Mary*, which had come round from Rye the preceding day, and was safely moored in the commodious refuge of this port, waiting my arrival.

The following afternoon, a light breeze from the southward, together with a favourable tide, enabled us to get out to sea, but alas! we might as well have remained in the harbour, for the wind soon after died away and our little bark (of 40 tons) drifted so much to the eastward, that by morning we found ourselves obliged to anchor off the North Foreland.

Under such circumstances almost any wind was better than none, and we hailed the approach (a few hours afterwards) of a breeze east north east, as with that we could beat about, and, if we gained nothing on our different tacks, we should at least maintain our ground, and be ready for some "more favouring gale."

Happily for us, Æolus and Phoebus did not this day act with their usual concordance, for as the latter descended towards the west, the former veered more and more to the east, and at length blew so steadily from the north east, that before the following midnight we were abreast of Ostend. Fortunately the light was hoisted which indicated there being water enough to admit of vessels passing the bar, but, to make doubly sure, we allowed a little sloop (which it seems had left Dover that morning) to take precedence of us, and seeing she met no obstacles, we were soon after her safely anchored in the harbour of Ostend.

Of this port I feel that I had better not say much, because I saw and know so little. I may nevertheless be permitted to remark, that on no occasion did I ever remember to have observed the coruscation of sparkling light so brilliant as it appeared here (round our little vessel) the preceding night. As Capt. Clarke justly remarked, this effect is very prevalent in the Mediterranean and Adriatic seas, but he added, that his memory could adduce no instance even there of its being so very vivid as on the present occasion.

To me, who had been roused from my bed of sickness by the flashes of light through the cabin windows, there appeared no doubt of the *Mary* being in flames; and even when I jumped on deck with a view to fly from the warm embraces of one all-devouring element to the cooler bosom of another, it was some time before my scattered senses could believe (what one of the sailors somewhat vulgarly, perhaps, but still very appositely remarked), "that by so doing, I should have only left the frying-pan for the fire!"

It seemed, indeed, as though the prow of our little vessel was boldly ploughing its way through a sea of phosphorus, undaunted and unhurt—but enough of these reflections—they can concern no one.

The day on which I first trod the Belgic shore was certainly inauspicious, being both wet and cold; but such are the delights of getting on *terra firma,* that after reaching the inn, changing my dress (which I had worn 36 hours), and obtaining a good breakfast at the Hotel d'Angleterre, I really fancied the climate delightful, nor could I help thinking of the lines in which Sheridan so cleverly celebrated the effects of a strong glass of brandy and water, on the system of the Prince Regent, *viz.*:—

The Prince exclaim'd ''tis very cold,'
And straight was brought the rummer;
When Swallow after Swallow came,
'And now,' says he, ''tis summer.'

However, what is called in England a sort of drizzling rain prevailed here all day, and towards evening produced in us some very aguish symptoms of alternate heat and cold. For these sensations our jolly landlady, (who was also our countrywoman), prescribed a bottle of Burgundy; and I must confess the remedy proved no less pleasing than efficacious; so that we noted down—Mem. "Burgundy, being as cheap as Port wine at Ostend, is equally good for the ague." To dwell so long upon anything connected with eating and drinking must, I fear, have a bad look to those who have never been to sea; but all others will admit how irresistibly these matters become the chief considerations of the first day ashore after a voyage. Let none, therefore, too hastily or harshly condemn any indulgence in these reflections.

For instance: I thought this fact fully extenuated innkeepers, both at home and abroad, for pitching their charges at a higher rate than at the inland towns, as certainly one does eat more during a few days after landing than for a fortnight afterwards.

"Aye! but," said my companions, "we drink in proportion, and there consists the landlord's chief profit!"

"Besides," added Mr. M., "remember how little we consumed previous to our embarkation at Ramsgate!" These arguments were too true to be contested.

During our saunter round the town, I could not help remarking that, although really very well paved, the streets appeared to be floating in water. However, of this seeming local disadvantage, the Duke of Wellington, like most of his military predecessors, had availed himself by keeping the sluices filled, and ready to inundate the surrounding country in case of an enemy's approach, at a moment's notice.

On the ramparts there were some beautiful pieces of artillery, manufactured at Tournay, and our vanity was somewhat gratified by seeing the duty of sentries performed there by British soldiers.

The harbour, also, which is about a quarter of a mile from the town and basin, was filled with English transports that had brought over many of our troops from America and other ports, and whom we saw parading like veterans about the streets. By the way, I was somewhat surprised to remark that the Belgians still retained the names given to their streets by their recent masters, such as *Rue de l'Empereur*, *Rue de Marie Louise*, &c, &c. The large square is also called the *Place d'Armes*, and it seems the centre from whence the streets diverge in different directions.

The *Hotel Imperiale* was considered the first inn here, but this was to be eclipsed by a magnificent building commenced on the quay some years since, and intended to be called *L'Hotel de Commerce*. So ignorant, however, were (or affected to be) the people of Ostend, that none of them could inform me why this undertaking was discontinued.

But Ostend has ever been subject to so many changes, that the mere fact of the inhabitants beginning to build any edifice at all is surprising.

On the afternoon of the 10th of June we walked a mile to a place called Sas, where the Canal of Bruges opens, supplied from the sea, and navigable for ships of 300 tons, and there we found a great number of British, Dutch, French, Belgians, Scotch, and Irish, all waiting as well as ourselves to embark in the *Treck scuyt*, or barge, for Bruges, a distance of twelve miles. In the whole there might be fifty passengers, and the weather becoming fine, it was altogether a most enlivening scene, when cheered by some wandering musicians. We were towed along by two half-starved horses, that derived but slight assistance from "the gentle breezes" while dragging us for four hours to our destination.

On reaching Bruges we could scarcely land ourselves in safety, much less our baggage, owing to the immense number of boys, men, and porters, who were quarrelling for the honour and privilege of conducting us to the inns, that they might be paid for doing so. Being a party of three, we deemed it most prudent to hire one of the hack coaches (in attendance), and each taking his own portmanteau to it, we triumphantly drove away from our assailants to the *Hotel de Commerce*—an inn of which we had no reason to complain, although report says the *Fleur de Blois* or the British Hotel are better.

Bruges was once the most flourishing city of Europe for trade, and it is said to be the place from whence the first bill of exchange was ever drawn. Amsterdam and Antwerp, however, soon proved the dangerous mercantile rivals they have since continued.

From the number of streets we saw during our short stay here, I can easily believe there were (as recorded) in the whole 260, besides six large squares, and the 200 bridges which cross the canals in so many directions, and are said to have given the name to the place.

The churches here are very fine, and all abounded with fine paintings previous to the incursions of the French; and even enough now remain to perpetuate the glory of their native artists. We had only time to visit the church of Notre Dame, and to admire the celebrated tombs of Charles the Hardy, Duke of Burgundy, who was killed at the battle of Nantz in 1477, and of his daughter Mary. They are of brass, gilt, and beautifully enamelled. Early in the French Revolution these splendid specimens of sculpture were concealed, and consequently preserved, by a verger, for whose head Robespierre offered 200 ducats; but Buonaparte, after his marriage with Marie Louise (daughter of the Emperor of Austria), visited this church, and, out of compliment to his illustrious consort, ordered it to be restored, and the verger was also handsomely rewarded for his fidelity.

The Grammar Schools in Bruges I found were still numerous; indeed for £20 *per annum* a lad might be taught every language and science, while, if his merit proved pre-eminent, he had a chance of being sent to college at the expense of the school.

It was melancholy to observe how many fine buildings had been destroyed during the French Revolution, but that this was perpetrated by the revolutionists for the purpose of making saltpetre for gunpowder from the incrustation of these ancient walls, was scarcely to be credited. Nevertheless, as we could not deny the fact, we bowed to the solemn asseveration of our guide and informant.

I should be wanting in gallantry, perhaps, to quit Bruges without adding that it seemed to abound with beautiful women, and chiefly among the lower classes, *grisettes,* &c.

June 11.—After taking one cup of good coffee, instead of three of inferior quality, as in England, we embarked by nine o'clock in the *Treck scuyt* for Ghent. It was considerably larger than the vessel which conveyed us to Bruges from Ostend, and had on board an immense assemblage of passengers, consisting of representatives from almost all European states. About two o'clock dinner was announced, consisting of three courses, all well dressed and excellent, and which I should remark was included in the five francs paid for our passage. For the dessert, wine, coffee or tea, of course we paid extra; and upon these extras I should think could alone rest the provider's profit. Nearly fifty of the most respectable passengers sat down to dinner, while the poor musicians regaled us with the "Troubadour," and thus earned their meal, as I presume they did their passage.

Ghent, or Gand.—The celebrated city of Ghent, at the end of the straight canal on which we were proceeding, had a very pleasing and somewhat imposing appearance. On the banks, too, between the avenues of trees and the water, the worthy citizens and their families were parading in various groups and considerable numbers. It being the Sabbath, they were arrayed in their best attire, which indeed appeared to have been manufactured in the days of Charles the Fifth rather than the reign of their Anglicised Prince of Orange. Interspersed among them were many French Royalists, both military and civil, who were doubtless the attendants of their king, who had sought a temporary asylum in Ghent. The gates were, nevertheless, guarded by British soldiers, but to the Flemish authorities we showed our passports, and were then led with great civility to the *Hotel de Flandre*, which, although a second-rate compared with the *Hotel de Lion d'Or, or l'Hotel d'Angleterre*, was overflowing with guests. However, Englishmen were not to be turned away in these times, and two French *emigres* who arrived a few moments before us, soon received the answer for which they were waiting, *viz.*, that the house was full. So it was, no doubt, by the time we had occupied three bed rooms, but I suspect not before.

We were fortunately early enough to join the promenade of company in the great square, and which consisted of a mixed assemblage of princes and peasants, generals and soldiers, with their female companions—all indiscriminately enjoying their evening lounge. Among the most conspicuous were the Duke of Felton, accompanied by a son of Victor, Duke of Belluno, and the Marshal de Bournville; Lord Hill, and several English officers, and Lord Courtenay, attended by a young lad, whom he was leading by the hand.

The lime trees which were planted round this large square shed a delightful fragrance; and as the gay coffee-houses were lighted up behind them, the scene became very agreeable and interesting.

The theatre was also open this evening, and unusually well filled; nor was the house or the acting without merit.

I forgot to observe that we saw Louis the Eighteenth dining, as it is justly called, "in public;" for the windows of his room were thrown open to the populace, who were eagerly staring at him as he sat surrounded by about 30 officers, enjoying, or affecting to enjoy, better appetites than under such circumstances might have been expected. His residence was a very respectable one, and had a peculiarly modern or English appearance.

His Majesty Louis the Eighteenth, however, could not feel so much at ease as he looked; for, perhaps conscious of the weakness of the citadel of Ghent, he had engaged all the post horses in the town, to be ready to carry him away the moment there should appear to be any necessity for retreating. We had little thought just then how near such a danger was at hand, else perhaps we should have lost sight of even the few (among the many) interesting objects which are to be seen at Ghent. The circumference of the city, indeed, was so great (about 15 miles), that Charles the Fifth might well pun upon the name of his native place, and tell Francis of France "he had a glove (*Gand*) in Belgium that would hold all the capital of the French monarch within it." Being intersected also with the rivers Scheldt, Lys, and Lieve, which run through it like so many canals, this place, as well as Bruges, abounds in bridges.

In the churches and chapels there were abundance of fine pictures and monuments; for the French seem here to have deposited most of the valuables plundered by them from surrounding provinces, Holland, &c. The cathedral contains a very fine painting of "the Crucifixion," by Vandyke, together with "the Discovery of the True Cross," by Polenck, who is I believe a native of this place, but had then left for Brussels to take the portraits of the Royal Family of Nassau. Whether the invitation on the part of the King of the Netherlands arose from vanity, or a desire to cultivate the arts, his friends and enemies were disputing. They, too, may settle the point.

For one like myself, who can so ill describe their beauties or defects, to enumerate paintings, would be both affectation and waste of time, although there were certainly many more worthy of attention. I may, however, observe that the Ascension of the Virgin Mary, by Francois, of Brussels (and who received 1500 florins for his work about three years after), and another representation of the same subject by Salm, who is now 70 years of age, and who only completed his task four years ago, tend to show that the fine arts have not quite abandoned their once most favoured home. Indeed, the execution of this latter picture appeared to better judges than myself to be "most masterly and chaste, while the truly heavenly countenance of the Virgin would do credit to the taste and judgment of any master."

Of the excellent botanical garden, we had just time to take a passing view; but from the public Library, formerly the Monastery of St. Bernard, we could not so easily withdraw ourselves. The good deeds of the saint himself afforded many subjects for some very excellent sculpture, and beside these were some fine busts of Vandyke, Rubens, Erasmus, and several other eminent men whom the Low Countries have produced. The length of the Library was 250 feet by 30 broad; and from the few specimens we saw of ancient works (some of them written by monks in the 14th and 15th centuries), I should infer that it contained a valuable collection.

On returning, after this ramble, to our inn, we found the diligence would set off that evening for Brussels about nine o'clock; and but for the peculiar appearance of our hotel, which we recognized when we thought it a mile off, we should perhaps have been left behind.

Merely adding, then, that this place gave birth to John of Gaunt, Duke of Lancaster, I believe I have exhausted all my notes worth transcribing, and I shall proceed with the reader along the straight and well-paved causeway to Alost, where we arrived at midnight, and therefore saw little more there than a wretched inn and a bad supper. We did, however, remark that the country between this place and Brussels was extremely fertile; abounding with lofty corn and luxuriant hops, the latter of which were carefully preserved from blight by the protection of a wooden cross conspicuously elevated to the top of one of the highest poles.

At break of day our coachman stopped for the fifth time in 30 miles to bait his horses (for I must do the Flemings the justice to say they treat their animals with great kindness, feeding them oftener than they flog them); and we were saluted by a bevy of little ragged children, who, like the youthful rogues in some parts of England, tumbled and ran along the road by the side of our diligence (a carriage far more suitable for such exhibitions than the royal mails of Great Britain), occasionally singing the most ludicrous compositions imaginable, but evidently intended to catch the ears of passengers of all nations. On discovering we were most of us English, they vociferated "*Vivent les Anglais!*" "*De Ainglishman goot mang!* He drink of *de* gin, and *loaf de Vrows!*" "*Vivent les Anglais!*" "Death to Napoleon!" "*Donnez moi d'argent!*" "Give havepennies!"

How such discordant words could be set to music I am at a loss to guess. However, so they were; and I hear form the leading sentiments of a popular and patriotic ballad in Belgium.

Before we reached Brussels, which we did about nine, the country seemed yet to become more fertile; and perhaps no city in Europe, unless it be Naples or Genoa, makes so fine an appearance at a distance, it being situated on the brow of a hill. The houses at the foot are, as in most suburbs, inferior; but they continued gradually to improve until we reached the summit, where is most appropriately placed the Grand Square, or Place Royale. I think in elegance this rivals any of our London squares, and is full as large as any of them, having a very beautiful garden and public walks in the centre.

On the different sides are magnificent buildings, such as the Palace of the King, and a fine church, of chaste architecture. At the various corners of the square are porticoes, surmounted with very appropriate statues, that give to the whole a most imposing effect. Hereabouts, too, are some excellent inns, much frequented by foreigners, who, I should think, may altogether find Brussels a very healthy, cheap, and agreeable residence.

I forgot before to observe that in the hotels during almost every meal, but at dinner particularly, we were regaled by music from the Savoyards, who unceremoniously entered our apartment, and commenced their tunes, trusting to our liberality for a reward of a few *sous* each. I confess this novelty was agreeable, and certainly, as Prince Eugene used to say of it—"*Cela vous evite la peine de parler.*"

It was, then, the 13th of June (for dates are beginning to grow important) when we found ourselves much better accommodated at the Hotel d'Hollande, in Brussels, than might have been expected, considering there were from 5000 to 8000 troops quartered in the town, besides the Duke of Wellington, his staff, and an amazing number of English visitors.

Little thinking, however, that there would be any necessity for haste, we rested this day at the inn for the purpose of recruiting ourselves, and hearing the news from the armies, with which almost every English, or indeed I might add, every man, seemed to be furnished in small portions, that he professed to retail out only to his neighbours, but loud enough to be heard throughout the coffee room where we were. Not the wisest among them seemed to anticipate any advance on the part of the French for several weeks at least; nor to us, as we afterwards strolled out, did

The pale-fac'd moon look bloody on the earth,
Or lean-look'd prophets whisper fearful change;

but all was quiet in the streets. On the following morning, therefore, being the 14th of June, we leisurely commenced our ramble through the town, and were first shown the Cathedral, which is built on an eminence, and thus conspicuous, naturally attracts the earliest attention of strangers. It is near the Gate of Louvain, and is I believe dedicated to a Saint Gudule, whose name I had never the honour of hearing before in any catholic country, and therefore notice it here, that if wrong, some friendly Christian may correct me.

Of the paintings in this church I forbear saying anything more than that they were many of them very fine, and worthy the attention of amateurs. So are the numerous monuments and painted windows. The latter were preserved from being wantonly destroyed by the French through the ingenuity of the Belgians, who, covering them over with temporary whitewash, made them resemble walls, and thus they escaped the notice of the destroyers.

As we were proceeding afterwards to the Botanical Garden, that hardly deserved notice, a cart obstructed our way, which the driver seemed resolved to make us notice; so sitting down, we indulged him for about ten minutes, when with great *sang froid* he advanced. It appeared to us a kind of market waggon, having no pole whereby the progress of the vehicle can be impeded in descending a hill, the driver is obliged to place his foot against the hind quarters of the horse, and preserve at the same time a very uncomfortable seat on a most precarious edge of the cart. How strange that they should not have been sensible to the many advantages so evident in the poles and harness of our English chaises and waggons, which they were passing every instant. But I suppose the countrymen here are like many of those in England—bigoted to blindness by habit.

In the Museum was a collection that did credit to the place, but which I had neither inclination more particularly to examine this morning, nor perhaps should I have when able more correctly to describe it, even though circumstances had not precluded our visiting this attractive spot again, and thus confirmed the impropriety of postponing till tomorrow what can be done today.

The *Stadthouse* is conveniently situate in the centre of Brussels, and close to their great vegetable market; it is a very ancient structure, and gratified our curiosity as much as anything we saw in the town.

My remaining notes for the day state only that the two theatres were both at the time closed, and that the women of the lower orders wore black woollen mantillas or cloaks, as in Spain.

On the 15th of June we had been chiefly occupied in seeing the various fountains by which Brussels is so admirably supplied with water, and we also visited one of the lace warehouses.

About six in the afternoon, while taking our coffee in the public room of the Hotel d'Hollande, an officer entered, and having seated himself in the next box to us, seemed fully as desirous of proving communicative, as *I* felt inquisitive to know, who he was and whence he came. My astonishment, then, may well be conceived when he represented himself to be an *aide-de-camp* to the Prince of Orange (I understood), and just arrived with dispatches for the Duke of Wellington, announcing "the advance of the French upon Charleroy, about 30 miles from Brussels, and their victory over the Prussians there!!"

But if I, who knew little of military affairs, felt surprised at such a communication, or the improbabilities of so sudden a movement on the part of Napoleon, what must have been the electric effect it produced on the minds of six or eight English officers who surrounded us, and who affirmed that the news must be impossible? Indeed, a Colonel ——, who sat nearest me, quietly insinuated that the quantity of Champagne which the Belgian officer had placed within his belt was beginning to affect his head. Nay, more; he added, that were such information in the Duke's possession, he, Colonel ——, should be one of the first to know it!

Now, whether this gentleman was copying the prudent reserve of his great master in such moments (for there were several subalterns present, who afterwards admitted that this was the conduct of the Duke when in Spain) I am still doubtful. Subsequent facts, however, gave to this latter conclusion a greater air of probability than to the idea that Colonel —— was ignorant of such a messenger having reached headquarters.

After discussing the matter with my communicative "*aide-de-camp*" for nearly an hour (while the surrounding guests seemed comparing us to Trim and Uncle Toby, so minutely were the different fortifications described, and so correctly, as it afterwards proved, did he detail every particular of the late battles), I proposed a walk in the park, to which the Belgian assented, remarking, however, as he went out, and with a significance that I dare say some of the poor fellows thought of in their last moments—for several of them were killed or wounded the next day—"Ah! gentlemen, you may laugh now, but many of your smiles may be changed to groans tomorrow."

I have dwelt a little upon this occurrence, because it seems in a great measure to refute a prevalent opinion in England—that the Duke of Wellington was taken by surprise about twelve o'clock in the night of the fifteenth, though at the Duchess of Richmond's ball; while the inhabitants, and perhaps most of the troops in Brussels *were* surprised I not only admit, but even expect my simple narrative will almost prove.

It was nearly eight o'clock in the evening when we reached the public promenade in the Park, and one of the first persons we saw was the Duke of Wellington, habited in a blue great coat and cocked hat, carrying an umbrella, although the weather was quite fine, and leaning on the arm of the Spanish General Alava, both of them evidently engrossed in earnest conversation, but. still not sufficiently so to entirely remove our doubts of the Belgian's report being somewhat premature; and I think I see his Grace illustrating

Those still and mental parts
That do contrive how many hands shall strike
When fitness calls them on.

There were also some members of the Duke of Richmond's family promenading leisurely about the gardens, and most of the military in Brussels were sauntering along the square, quite unconcerned. Two brothers of the Prince of Orange, rather smart looking young officers, appeared far more deeply engaged by the lively tune the band was there playing than by any thoughts of the martial music of the morrow.

Thus, then, everything tended to increase our want of faith in the extraordinary intelligence chance had brought to our ears; but when we saw the company proceeding to the Duchess of Richmond's ball, we no longer hesitated to return to our quarters and join in the laugh, which was too easily raised by some of the subalterns at the expense of our imaginary credulity.

Scarcely, however, had the clock struck twelve, when I was roused from my slumbers by a violent knocking at the door, accompanied by cheering exclamations from the well-known voices of my two fellow-travellers of "Get up, Smith, directly: there's the devil to pay in the town!" "The troops are all repairing to the rendezvous! The bugles are sounding to arms in every direction, and it is believed the French are at hand!!"

Well might they conclude with such an opinion, and no one believed it more truly than myself. However, these were no moments for hesitation: having, therefore, very hastily dressed myself, I joined my companions in the courtyard below, where so many of all nations, all sizes, and all colours, had assembled, each clamouring to know what was the matter, that it was an affair of some difficulty to distinguish whether we were surrounded by friends or foes.

A most persevering bagpiper had taken his station near the door of our hotel (because, as we conjectured, it was the quarter where so many Highlanders were billeted), and he seemed resolved not to cease playing till his countrymen were thoroughly roused to arms. How well he succeeded was evident, for on sallying into the street we perceived the tartan dresses coming regularly and quietly out of many of the neighbouring houses, and proceeding to a point whither our curiosity induced us to follow. The night was excessively dark, and the lamps (if there had been any), were already extinguished. The stillness that prevailed as we passed through the streets was occasionally disturbed by the trampling of horses, already led out to be caparisoned, and the rattling of muskets or sabres "now fitting for the fight."

The first information we obtained was from an English soldier, to whom we became suddenly introduced by his having nearly upset us as he bolted out of one of the doors we were passing, with his musket on his shoulder, and a heavy knapsack behind him. Nor was his intelligence other than consolatory to us poor ignorant amateurs (for such, amid so many warriors, I fancied we looked like), as he stated that the Duke had ordered the drums to beat to arms at midnight, and the troops quartered in Brussels to the rendezvous in the Place Royale by three in the morning.

Thus, then, we ventured to infer, that if the French were really very near, his Grace could hardly have afforded so much leisure to prepare. Boldly, therefore, did we now proceed to this appointed place; and never while I exist can the impressions which the succeeding three hours created there, be effaced from my memory. Every second of them was to me of the most intense interest. This scene, too, was, I almost suspect, as peculiar to my two companions as it was indeed novel to me; for except those who were actually connected with the army, and consequently were rather actors than observers, scarcely any English were here much before the troops began their march. Before they go, however, I will endeavour to enumerate some of their expressions, looks, and actions, in all of which I confess myself to have felt a sympathy almost equal to the original feeling from whence it sprung.

By far the most conspicuous undoubtedly were the Highlanders, whose lofty caps of fur, and shorter kilts of plaid, were contrasts not very common in this country. In justice, however, to every countenance I scrutinized, whether Scotch, English, or Irish, I must confess that I could discover nothing like the workings of fear, although I fancied I did read on many an intelligent face the various reflections of the mind. Some were silently eating their hard biscuits, while others spoke out. The first and foremost among the latter was an Hibernian officer, who, while coolly sharpening his sword against the wall, said—

"Ah, well, never mind! I've no doubt we'll make short work of the business wherever we may be after going to, and if so, why surely we may get drunk when it's over!"

"To be sure ye may," answered a Highlander, "but I suspect Master Bonie wud 'na made tha furst hit had na ben pratty strong, mun, an weel prepared for a gude fight."

"Well, dam; Ar care noot" exclaimed a north country man, who was sitting on his knapsack, "hoo that be, nor when, sor it tak place, and sor it but prove warm while ut lasts."

"Farewell, my good fellow," said Major —— to his friend at parting, "give my affectionate love to Ellen; tell her where I am gone, and that if I fall it shall be in the paths of glory." ,

"Egad," cried a lively young subaltern, who I think was Welch from his dialect, "jest as I was about to dance with a sweet pretty wench at the Duchess of Richmond's ball last night, I heard Wellington bid us go to our quarters directly, where we should hear something 'interesting.' Interesting enough, faith, it was too!"

Now, as I believe there can be no doubt that the Duke of Wellington *did* attend the above entertainment, so I think nothing more probable than that one who so often took his officers by surprise in Spain, should do so again in Brussels. The sequel, however, will show that his Grace had been many hours preparing himself. The place of rendezvous being almost within sight of the Duchess of Richmond's residence, the dawning of day exposed many a military man coming from the gay scene in too much haste to change his habiliments of the ball for those of the battle. Many, therefore, fell this day (16th of June) in the silk stockings wherein they had but the preceding evening decked themselves for the enjoyments of life. What a train of reflections might arise from this circumstance! But the bustle was beginning to increase too much for quiet meditations.

It was now four o'clock, and already the various regiments quartered about Brussels had assembled in the Place Royale, and consisting of, I believe, the 92nd, 32nd, 79th, 28th, 18th, 44th, and 42nd, besides the artillery. All waited in awful suspense "the word," which was soon given—to march! and even now my blood thrills at the recollection of the sound; but how shall I describe the effect produced by the cheers of the crowd which had assembled to see the departure of their friends, their relatives, and defenders? *My pen must fail, though others may succeed*: I will, therefore, only observe that the sun was just appearing above the horizon as the march began; and it was by a winding descent that we beheld those brave fellows proceeding with a cheerful air to their unknown destination.

The Highland regiments were preceded by their bagpipers, and the others by martial music from their bands—the arms of all glittering through the trees. In vain did the sentries endeavour to keep back the women who desired, but were forbidden, to follow their husbands to the field. Some darted forward in spite of the bayonets, and, eluding every effort to overtake them, continued to attend the army, to assist in battle, and to succour in distress, those to whom they belonged. Indeed, several fell victims to their devotion, being shot (let us hope by chance) as they too heedlessly passed between the hostile ranks. In poor Keats's words, I thought—

How glorious this affection for the cause
Of stedfast valour, toiling gallantly.

By five o'clock in the morning of the 16th of June all the troops had quitted Brussels, and

Nought but a solemn stillness left.

The Duke followed about an hour afterwards, and at nine o'clock I felt a stronger inclination than my companions to accompany two other amateurs to or near the scene of action. In vain, however, were all my efforts to buy, beg, hire, or steal a horse for the occasion, every one having been so strictly engaged for the use of the army, that my friends had some difficulty in preserving those which belonged to them. As it often happens, therefore, what I then thought the bane of all my reputation as a traveller, I have since considered as the salvation of my life and property as a man; for by two o'clock the firing of artillery proved the engagement to be warmer and nearer to us than would have suited my convenience and taste. Indeed, so loud was the roaring of cannon, that my fellow-travellers insisted, with becoming prudence, on our securing a conveyance to take us to Ghent, where we arrived that evening, doubtful if the French might not (if victorious) get there by a short cut before us.

Happily we found no such hosts there to receive us; but Louis the Eighteenth was still at his old asylum, waiting, nevertheless, in such awful suspense for information, and so much better prepared (with carriages, not legs) to run away than ourselves, that after holding a council of war, in which I was again outvoted by my wiser partners in the triumvirate, it was resolved we should proceed by the barge next morning towards Bruges, not only because that was on the high road to Ostend, where our vessel lay, but because, on further inquiry, we found King Louis's destination, in case of need, was Antwerp, and that His Majesty's horses were kept harnessed for the purpose of starting at a moment's notice, with a cavalcade of attendants that might impede the progress of others on the same road, besides attracting the peculiar attention of all the pursuers on that route. No sooner, however, had we reached Bruges, than so many reports—

Blown by surmises, jealousies, or conjectures—

had overtaken us with regard to the success of the allied armies, that we could hardly feel ourselves safe until actually at the same port with our little sloop. At Ostend we accordingly arrived once more, on the morning of the ever-memorable 18th of June. There we had not been seated many hours before we were shown the extract of a letter, said to have been just received by Colonel Gregory (Commandant at Ostend), from either Louis the Eighteenth, or the Duke of Wellington himself. I give it *verbatim*:—

Buonaparte has been completely defeated at Gemappe. The battle was very bloody. General Pack is killed. The English division have suffered severely. The Duke of Brunswick was killed at the head of the Brunswickers.

Mem.—The Duke writes this from the field of battle, and he is in pursuit of Buonaparte, with General Blucher. The Belgian troops conducted themselves remarkably well.

After a bulletin so apparently official and decisive, it will not be wondered at that Ostend should be all gaiety, glory, and rejoicing, or that, in the pride of our hearts as Englishmen, we should courageously resolve to retrace our steps towards that scene from whence We had just come in fearful doubts of any such result. If we had embarked immediately, we should have borne the first intelligence to

England. How fortunate for us that this premature intelligence, founded on the events of the 16th, was confirmed by that of the 18th; else we should most surely have met the retreating and the conquering armies from which we had taken such prudent measures to escape; for on the 19th of June, at half-past four, a.m., we were again on board our old *Treck sckuyt* for Bruges and Ghent.

We reached the latter place at five that afternoon, and there learned for the first time that the grand, the bloody, and decisive battle in which the allies were victorious, had only taken place the day before! To this account many added that the Duke of Wellington had nearly been defeated. Without entering much into these particulars, therefore, we cordially sympathized in the general joy which a different result seemed so universally to produce. We toasted his Grace in a bumper of Burgundy, and then proceeded to take a peep at Louis, who was doing the same, doubtless with equal sincerity.

A diligence being about to set off for Brussels this evening, we resolved to make up for our former retreat (which, compared with those made by other amateurs to Antwerp on the 17th inst., might be considered a masterly one), by being among the first to contemplate the scene of action. Whether the poor beasts which now dragged our diligence along had been jaded by their recent unusual occupation, or whether the roads were rendered bad by unusual traffic, the darkness of the night did not permit us to observe; but we were twelve hours performing a distance of thirty miles, and the sun was already high before we entered Brussels. Alas, how changed was the appearance of this place since we left it!

It was on the 20th of June we arrived at the barriers of Brussels, where we met several carts with our wounded countrymen or their prisoners; but we could scarcely pass some of the main streets from the crowds of both either resting against the walls, or slowly moving about, as their wounds permitted. Fortunately the weather was now fine, and the warm fresh air far more favourable to invalids than close rooms. Nevertheless, we understood that all the hospitals were overflowing, and every private residence was occupied by them.

At the door of each house that we passed, the women were busily occupied preparing lint for the wounds of their suffering guests within; and among the trees near the park were about 200 of those magnificent horses belonging to the Scots Greys, which were considered to be mortally wounded, but did not look so, or seemed conscious of their own state.

On reaching our old quarters, the *Hotel d'Hollande*, we found the rooms all occupied, and the courtyard strewed with straw for the accommodation of wounded soldiers. Of course we were resolved to seek a lodging elsewhere rather than propose to be admitted where we might possibly disturb any of these brave fellows. The landlord's daughters, however, who were very civil and intelligent, (and to whom, by the way, I owe a tribute of thanks for an offer they made during our former visit to pass me off as their cousin, and a Belgian, in case the French had taken Brussels), now suggested that we should find equal difficulty everywhere else, but that if we would put up with a couple of old rooms fitting up in the granary, we should at least have well-aired beds in them.

Such a bird in the hand, while proffered with so much civility, was irresistible, nor had we reason to repent accepting it. We returned, therefore, to our old coffee-room to take some refreshment, but how the scene was changed since we left the Belgian messenger and the sceptical subalterns there! Now, at almost every table sat a military man, with a bandaged limb and a sickly countenance, taking what sustenance the nature of his sufferings might permit.

One young Irishman alone seemed unhurt; but he looked deeply depressed, having, as he stated, seen the last of the three brothers who had entered the army with him at the commencement of the Peninsular war, fall by his side on the 18th. "Ah," said he, "'twill be my turn next."

A very handsome Hanoverian, who had been greatly disfigured by a back sabre cut across the bridge of his nose on the 16th, made light of his wound, and derived consolation from having brought down the runaway who inflicted it, with a pistol. The young German rather amused us by going over to the milliner's shop opposite three or four times a day, for the pretended purpose of buying bandages, and employing the young women to dress his wounds, while he, in return, most probably inflicted others less easily cured.

Generally speaking, indeed, the wounded men seem to vie with each other in bearing their agonies with fortitude; and we actually saw two British soldiers disputing the precedence of valour at some particular moment, one of whom had lost a leg, and the other was severely wounded in the arm !

The Duke of Wellington, we were told (for amid so much confusion I could neither ascertain the veracity of my information, any more than I will now vouch for the fidelity of my own relation of it, notwithstanding I desire only to detail what I did see and hear), had returned to Brussels to dine with those of his staff who were able to join him on the 19th (it was now the 20th) of June. Some who saw him said that he appeared to feel much grief for the dead, mingled with his joy for the victory, and that he acknowledged the Providential interference by which he himself had been preserved in the hour of battle.

We heard, also, that while at dinner, a French General who had been taken prisoner insisted upon seeing the Duke of Wellington, that he might communicate something of importance. He was therefore escorted by a guard into the presence of his Grace, when, being questioned by Col. Freemantle I believe, as to the object of his mission, the boasting Frenchman said he could speak to none but the commander-in-chief!

The Duke being then pointed out, *Monsieur* thus began:—

Sir: I appear before you as a General of France, who claims, on behalf of himself and his fellow prisoners, the attendance of the British surgeons, besides all the medical attendance which it is your *duty* to bestow upon us.

"Sir," replied the Duke of Wellington, almost without looking the insolent general in the face, "I have but too many of my own brave followers who are yet without surgical or medical attendance; you may therefore retire."

His Generalship did so, not a little abashed by this just rebuke, and those for whom he petitioned soon learnt that British clemency towards the vanquished was better produced by the natural feelings of the conquerors, than through the intervention of those leaders who had so long been the abettors of ferocity in other countries.

A number of Buonaparte's manifestos, dated Brussels, 20th of June, were found among his papers. With this exception, we heard nothing else today worth recording.

On the morning of the 21st of June we would fain have proceeded to view the field of battle, but could obtain no vehicle whatever, and no other animal than a little French cavalry horse, which was offered to me by his captor for a *louis*; but as it appeared scarcely strong enough to carry one, we thought it would ill suit three of us. We had, therefore, another day to prepare ourselves (among the less dreadful objects in Brussels) for seeing the more sanguinary plains of Waterloo. Thus, too, we were able to visit some of the crowded hospitals, where the very floors seemed strewed with the wounded, the dying, and the dead, indiscriminately collected from all nations, whose sons had been engaged in the late conflict.

I can never forget one poor unfortunate, to whom, when my benevolent companion was about distributing in turn our little stock of cake and wine, hesitated for several minutes to receive any, although evidently gasping for want of nourishment. At length, looking us in the face, he exclaimed, "*Non, Messieurs; vous vous trompez; je suis Francais moi.*" As much as to say, "I see you come here to succour your own countrymen, or at most their allies, but certainly not their enemies. *I* will not, therefore, rob them of what is their due, besides being most undeservedly sheltered in your hospital!!"

Need I describe the effect produced upon our minds by the magnanimous conduct of this poor Frenchman, or say that the consequences were his having a double allowance, with our best wishes for his recovery ?

In the streets we met several French prisoners being brought in by Belgians, and compared with the trim of their escort (whose jackets, I must say, appeared but little soiled), the former cut but wretched figures with their wounds and dirty rags. Here and there a stray member of the "Invincibles," or more properly the Imperial Guard, was distinguished from the others by his long coat, with the letter N on its flaps, and I think I might safely add, by the peculiar sullenness of his looks. It seemed to us as though, conscious of their boasts, they would rather have died (nor did these brave men by all accounts shun death) than be thus led as objects of derision to those whom they held in such contempt, or to whom they had declared themselves invincible!

A few were also pointed out to us as having been caught

exchanging the national cockade that was on the *exterior,* for the white one they had carefully preserved in the *inside* of their caps!—a *ruse de guerre,* indeed, and one which, perhaps, under all circumstances, was very excusable. At all events, they were in our eyes objects of pity rather than of ridicule; knowing, as we did, how many poor fellows were dragged into the ranks of a man by whose conscription they had suffered, and that they only wanted the opportunity to serve their legitimate king, and to restore peace to the country. Nevertheless there were all sorts, for while one prisoner showed me the very buttons of Louis the Eighteenth, in which he swore they had forced him to fight for Napoleon, another exulted in the tricks he had played the Royalists, *"pour l'amour de l'Empereur!"*

The little anecdotes of different officers and men who had signalized themselves during the late engagements were now beginning to crowd my memoranda book. One told us he had seen Lord Uxbridge's leg amputated, and that this nobleman not only bore the operation like a hero, but afterwards distributed his fine stud among his staff, observing, "it was pretty evident he should never be able to make another charge on their backs, and 'twas a pity they should be idle who had so long been accustomed to activity."

The same informant also added, that Colonel Hely had before saved the noble earl's life, by cutting down with his athletic arm a French dragoon, who was about to fire at his lordship's head. To be sure this was altogether to me a day

Of scenes most strange and dread;

for, on proceeding to my bedchamber at night I had to pass the body of General Picton, covered over with a sheet, except the face, which in death was still expressive, and but too plainly betrayed the course of the fatal shot that had passed from the upper side of the skull obliquely down to the opposite jaw, whence it was extracted, and shewn to us by his *aide-de-camp*, Capt. Tyler, who also pointed out a previous wound in the side. To the courtesy of this latter gentleman I was indebted for permission thus to contemplate the manly form of this valiant soldier, who fell on the 16th of June,

> . . . . leading up his division to a charge with bayonets, by which one of the most serious attacks made by the enemy was defeated.—*Vide Duke of Wellington's Dispatch.*

It being pretty well known that Sir Thomas Picton and the Duke of Wellington had been for some time at variance, we were particularly gratified to hear that his Grace had given special orders to have the body conveyed to England, and interred with all the honours due to so distinguished an officer.

The next day, therefore, a sort of *barouche* was hired for the purpose, and the corpse being placed in a coffin, was taken away by Capt. Tyler.

During the whole of the night I was disturbed from my slumbers by the noise caused by the undertakers who were most busily at work in the room beneath me. In passing, therefore, early to the chamber of my companions, I met Captain Tyler, giving some directions for the sale of two of Sir Thomas's horses, left at a place three miles from Brussels, when, being seized with a desire to possess such valuable relics, and further hoping they might enable us to follow the conquering armies to the gates of Paris, I agreed to give the apparently low price of 80 *Napoleons* for both the above chargers, which was accepted, and an order written by Captain T. for the delivery of them to me.

Again, however, was I doomed to see my valorous determinations frustrated; for on finding the groom in whose care they were left, he expressed his sincere regret at having, in consequence of his anxiety to get rid of them, accepted

70 *Napoleons* from another quarter, although, as he admitted, either horse was worth more money! What treasures they would have been in England!

The 22nd of June being now arrived, our curiosity to visit the field of battle could no longer be restrained. Having bargained, therefore, with a sort of hackney coachman to take us thither in one of those vehicles which ply about Brussels for the accommodation of passengers, we breakfasted at seven, and shortly afterwards set off. With what agitated feelings we did so, I leave those to imagine who have never yet visited such a scene in reality, or others to describe who, having done so often, can now remember their first impressions.

After passing along a paved way for nearly eight miles, skirted on each side by the Forest of Soigne, we arrived at the village of Waterloo about twelve o'clock, the celerity of our movements being greatly obstructed by the almost unbroken chain of carriages of every denomination which were bringing the wounded, the dying, and the dead, from "the ensanguined plain." The road was rendered dreadfully heavy by the immense ruts, after one of those torrents of rain which fell on the 17th, and Was so invariably the harbinger of the Duke of Wellington's greatest victories on the Peninsula. Every inch of our journey was nevertheless too interesting to appear tedious, and we were still sympathizing in the sufferings of those who had passed us when our postillion stopped at an inn, opposite to a neat little church, which became the sepulchre of numbers of valiant British heroes.

Without a cigar I found it impossible (so great was the effluvia) to visit the interior, where, lying on the straw, we found a few soldiers, so desperately wounded, that on our return in the evening, alas! three of them were no more, and the fourth was dying. Had we been in a state to take refreshment, the little inn (already crowded with better claimants to the landlord's attention), could not, I suspect, have afforded us any, and we should have thought ourselves wanting in humanity to consume a grain of that stock which was evidently but little enough among so many. Our horses, therefore, being fit to proceed, we readily attended the driver's summons, and continued along the main road, already strewed with broken carriages, &c, till we came to Mont St. Jean, two miles distant, the position upon which we were informed the English had fallen back after the engagement at Quatre Bras on the 16th.

On the doors of several houses as we passed along we observed, written in chalk, the number of "blesses" it contained, and sometimes the name of the regiments to which they belonged.

A little further, and we found ourselves on the great arena where the fate of Europe was decided. It seemed to me an open plain of about 20 miles in circumference, and most admirably adapted for the use to which it had been so lately devoted. Our driver, however, assured us, that but a week since the lofty corn was waving on the very ground where the marks of horses' hoofs, or ruts formed by the numerous waggons that had passed and were still passing, could alone now be discerned.

Numbers of *cuirasses*, bayonets, broken swords, saddles, caps, and feathers, already attracted our attention, soon, alas! to be occupied by still more saddening objects. The almost naked body of a soldier, over which a carriage had passed, lay on the side of the road, and not far off were several dead horses, looking more horrible to us from their positions, being on their backs, swollen and heavy with the rain, and their legs stiff in death.

We pursued our course towards *La Haye Sainte,* a solitary farm house, memorable for the importance attached to it by the Duke of Wellington and Buonaparte, as also for the desperate and successful effort made by the latter to obtain a position that he imagined would shake the British centre. Notwithstanding, however, that Napoleon so far attained his object, owing to the failure of the ammunition of its defenders (the German Legion), no material advantages accrued to the French in consequence. In fact, I strongly suspect Buonaparte was completely out-generaled all this day. It would be impossible to depict the countenances of the poor fellows (chiefly French) who were lying against the battered walls of *La Haye Sainte,* moaning in their miseries. In the interior we caught a glimpse of a heap of slain, and retired. We were not yet equal to such appalling sights—

Such horrid groans and dismal yells.

Near this spot we observed an unusual number of cuirasses scattered around, from which we presumed those "armour-bearers" met the British Horse Guards hereabouts, and that their iron cases were too weighty for the immediate plunder of those human wolves who had already so indecently despoiled the dead of everything else, and who, as Sheridan so justly described them,

Ever follow like vultures in the train of war,
To feed upon the blood of the brave.

Nay, more: at a little distance we plainly saw some men flaying the dead horses for the sake of their skins, and perhaps their flesh, which might have proved even nourishing food for many a starving prisoner at this critical juncture.

Lost in the contemplation of such sights as these, we jogged on to the still more memorable farmhouse called *La Belle Alliance.* It was here that the Duke of Wellington and Marshal Blucher were said (for the point is still doubtful) to have first met after the victory which their joint forces had accomplished, and to have embraced each other so cordially. If so, the singular and original appellation of this farm renders the coincidence more extraordinary, and the name still more appropriate than it would otherwise be.

It was a little above this spot that Napoleon remained during a great part of the battle, and in the hollow in front there must have been a desperate conflict, if we may judge from the immense number of bodies that lay heaped together. Indeed the very ditches were filled with them, and they were so slightly covered by the dirt thrown over them, that, mistaking it for plain ground, I was perfectly electrified as I found my own foot give way (in a sort of bog), to see another start up! It was fortunate that I was moving slowly, and had advanced no further; else I might in one moment have been out of sight of my companions, and buried among the heroes of Waterloo without participating in their glory.

My curiosity was a little blunted by this event; so, picking up a tolerably good cuirass, I put it into our carriage, and resumed my safe position there, hoping to bring home this relic and memento of the occurrence, which, however, some of the Belgian *gens d'armes* thought (and very justly) I should remember well enough without, and therefore took it from me afterwards, on entering Brussels.

We now found our way more than ever impeded by the dead bodies of horses and men; the broken or plundered ammunition carriages too, lay beside the road, which was in several places actually strewed with holsters, bayonets, and pieces of cloth, red, white, and blue. Just here, also, I was particularly struck with the position of a poor fellow who lay dead near us, with his face to the ground, and his arms and legs extended in such a manner as to make us infer that he died in agony, or, at all events, in the very act of "biting the dust." From his height and muscular figure (already nearly stripped), I suspect he had on the day of battle worn a large *cuirass*, which lay near him, shattered, either by the balls of the enemy or the hands of the plunderers.

Now, it certainly may be asked why I speak thus contemptuously of others for picking up what they could find, while we, and many more (though perhaps stimulated by less sordid motives) did the same thing in a minor degree? I answer, that *we* never stripped the dying, or otherwise hastened their death; we merely sought a sad memorial of Waterloo.

On our right a sort of scaffolding was pointed out that was thought to have been erected by Napoleon for the purpose of seeing the operations of the armies, but I still doubt this fact, and I am tolerably well assured he never used it for any such purpose. Nevertheless, the construction of this wood-work might well justify such an opinion, and at all events it would have served as a delightful stand for stewards to have seen the interesting contest of "France against all Europe." I did not hear, however, that any one occupied it on the occasion.

A little further on, our attention was drawn to the melancholy sight of a line of bodies, that appeared to have been mowed down by artillery; and while we were led by appearances to infer that they might be our countrymen, we could not but regret the imperious, but sad necessity which, calling all attention to the living, thus left so many heroes lying exposed upon the plain, and perhaps, even when buried, to be but slightly covered by the earth, in a spot not distinguished by any monumental record. Still, their names will be handed down to posterity by the despatches of their valiant chief, while, as a modern poet says:—

A tomb is theirs on every page,
An epitaph on every tongue,
The present hours, the future age,
For them bewail; to them belong.

We were now approaching the village of Gemappe, upon which the British army fell back after their severe *rencontre* with the French at Quatre Bras on the 16th, whence it is about six miles distant. Before this place we concluded (for without any military man or guide to invent or inform us, we could only *guess* at facts), the French must have planted the chief part of their abundant artillery on the 18th, as we observed so many pieces here in charge of some Prussian soldiers. On most of the cannon I remarked the letter N. very conspicuous, and the date of June, 1814. This was, I think, the period when Napoleon was himself an exile in Elba, and Louis the Eighteenth—King of France! Surely, then, if really manufactured when dated, there must have been some illicit foundry for the purpose, or the friends of Buonaparte were bolder in their measures than I could have believed.

One of the Prussian sentries here offered us a cabriolet, originally belonging to a French officer, for 25 *francs* (about a guinea!) but doubting his right to effect the sale (though the carriage was evidently worth £50 at least), and being, moreover, unable to take away our purchase at the moment, we declined accepting this tempting offer. The same difficulty, however, did not prevent our purchasing some black silk stockings, a fine cambric shirt, and a (Waterloo) blue neckkerchief;[1] a bargain was, therefore, soon struck, and the articles were divided by lot amongst us. The latter fell to my possession, and shall be retained by me or entrusted to safer hands, for the purpose of being viewed as a genuine trophy from the plains of Gemappe.

Chance afterwards leading me to open an artillery waggon, similar to what we had observed stuffed with balls or tow, I was surprised to find it filled with letters and newspapers, opened or sealed in a manner that led us to suppose this must have been the wily Napoleon's General Post-office for all communications to or from his army subsequent to its arrival in the Netherlands. The newspapers being dated

---

1. Now in the possession of my friend, Mrs. H. H., of Bedfordsquare.

the 8th of June, could not long have arrived in the camp. The Prussian sentry here told me I might peruse any of them, but carry none away; nor could my companions, by temptations of a peculiar nature, keep his head long turned aside from his duty.

The novel sight of an English coin, however, at length abstracted the honest fellow's attention long enough for me to put a few newspapers and letters in my pocket, and to shut down the lid of the box in a manner that led him to suppose my curiosity more easily gratified than it really was. One of the letters ran as follows :—

Tu ne dois pas douter, mon cher Alcibiade, du plaisir avec lequel j'ai recu ta lettre; je suis certainement tres loin de trouver mauvais que tu m'y donne le titre d'ami, je te prie au contraire de me continuer les sentimens que justifient ce titre, et de croire qu'ils sont sincerement partagés. Les reflexions que tu as faites avant ton départ son tres justes, mais il me semble qu'il t'en a echappé une et qui, a mon avis etait la plus determinante, c'est, qu'apres la manière dont tu avais annoncé ton opinion et l'attachment que tu avais temoigné pour Napoleon, il ne l'etait pas permis d'hesiter, et tu ne devais pas balancer a partir sans t'exposer, a etre tané de ne pas vouloir servir un parti auquel tu paraissais si devoué.

Tous ces motifs reunis et plus encore la vocation que tu parais avoir pour l'art militaire, tout te fait la loi de supporter avec patience les désagremens inséparables des commencements de la carrière que tu vas courir, et dont tu seras bien dedommagé si par ton zele, ton assiduété, tu parviens de l'avancement que t'est promis et que tu obtiendras indubitablement si tu as lé bon esprit de concilier la bienveillance de tes chefs. Ce pays ci est toujours dans le meme etat ou tu l'as laissé, la présence du commissaire extraordinaire n'a produit aucun effet; il parait que le sort des grand fonctionnaires publics est toujours d'être trompés, les administrations sont en gênerai

dans de mauvais principes, les Royalistes levent impuné-
ment la tête, et distillent leur venin en colportant les bruits
les plus absurds que sont recueillis par les gobes-mouches, et
tuent l'esprit public; il y a huit jours des jeune gens (d'ici)
que tu connais bien, en sortant d'un orgie ont vociferé le cri
de Vive le Roi! La police a dû en etre informé et il n'en est
rien resulté, cela ne t'etonnera pas, tu sais comment nous
sommes administrés. La ville que tu habites va devenir selon
les apparences, un théâtre important, tu me feras plaisir en
m'informant de ce que se passera d'important.

Comme les carabinièrs sont pres de toi, tache de voir Petit,
et faite lui de ma part des réproches sur le silence qu'il garde
visa-vis de moi, je sais que ton pere doit t'arrive aujourdhui,
ainsi je ne te dirai rien de ta famille.

  Adieu. Crois a l'amitié sincère de ton devoué.

            Petitgrande Fils. [2]

Time only permitted us to wait half-an-hour in Gemappe, while our horses were again refreshed; for, as I before said (and the trait is sufficiently honourable to be repeated), the Belgians take even more care of dumb animals
than of themselves. We therefore wandered about among
the shattered houses and sheds which, but for the numbers
of wounded, dying, and dead soldiers who lay within them,
would indeed have resembled a deserted village or a plundered hamlet. The little gardens were partly destroyed, and
the fields which but a few days before waved with luxuriant corn, now, alas! resembled a farmyard, trampled into
manure by horses and cattle of every description.

In a tolerably good room I recognized the British uniform on the fine figure of a man who, although walking
about, was evidently much wounded. He proved to be an
Irishman, and a private in the 14th Dragoons, who had
been pierced through the back by a Polish lancer at Quatre

---

2. The original is in the possession of my friend, Mr. F., of F——n, in Devonshire.

Bras, and so deeply had this instrument penetrated, that his chest was as black as his back was lacerated. The poor fellow took some pains to make us understand how such an apparently disgraceful scar was inevitable while surrounded by these lancers, and further, insinuated a hope that we did not suspect it had been done in a retreat! Of course, if we could have thought so, this was not the moment to acknowledge such sentiments; we, therefore, shook the brave soldier's other hand, in grateful acknowledgment of what he had done and was now suffering for his country, and having drunk success to the Allies out of our pocket pistol, we parted with sensations mutually agreeable.

Here and there we found a black Brunswicker lying about, and looking the more deplorable from his gloomy garb, and a skull in front of his military cap, on which I believe was inscribed "Death or Victory!" Alas! it was their misfortune to experience both in the loss of that princely hero, the Duke of Brunswick, who fell on the 15th, while leading them to the victory they assisted to achieve.

All, however, who could be recognized as allies, certainly experienced from the few remaining inhabitants of this little place every attention it was in their power to bestow. Nor were the wounded foes by any means neglected, although friends of course received the first consideration at the hands of those for whom they had fought and bled.

"*Allons, Messieurs, allons! tout est pret,*" exclaimed our postillion, who began to grow a little restless at our delay; and fearing, I suppose, that we should hardly reach Brussels before night, he reminded us that "we had *come* a long way that morning." From this we sagaciously inferred that we had a long way to go back, and therefore jumped once more into our fiacre, intending not to stop till we again reached Waterloo. A smoking pile, however, at the distance of about a quarter of a mile from the high road, excited so much discussion among us as to whether it could possibly be kindled to consume the innumerable bodies that were becoming almost putrescent on the field, that my companion, Mr. M., resolved to set the matter at rest by running to see it, while the carriage walked slowly on. Capt. C. and myself suggested the probability of his meeting some stragglers on the way, who might rob him, and leave his defenceless body among the dead, or consuming in the very flames which kindled such unusual courage in his breast.

Nevertheless, finding that curiosity predominated over reason, we resolved to follow him, but our desire to reach the goal being less keen, our pace perhaps was more slow, and Mr. M. had already headed us about 200 yards, when we suddenly beheld a Prussian hussar coming from behind a hill in front of our precipitate comrade, who then halted, and cast "a lingering look behind," as though he would fain rejoin one of us, now at equal distances from him, though at separate points from each other. A retreat, however, on his part, was as hazardous as an advance on ours, all of us being entirely unarmed.

Well, then, here we were, as another journalist (Simpson) somewhat sarcastically observes, three Englishmen about to be defeated by a single Prussian! but "*divide et impera*" was evidently the fellow's motto, from his watching this particular opportunity; and it must be our apology for submitting to the disgrace, if what was inevitable can be termed disgraceful at all. The Prussian lost not a moment in drawing his sabre, and making a thrust at Mr. M., who, falling instantly, I concluded he was killed, and consequently stood appalled, fearful of going up to him and ashamed to desert my comrade, notwithstanding there seemed to be every probability of my being soon sent by the robber to join him in another world!

In a few minutes, however, I was roused from this reverie by observing Mr. M. first rise upon one knee, in spite of the Prussian's repeated thrusts (as they then appeared to me, although it afterwards proved they were only pretended ones); then upon the other, and lastly, get upon his legs, and surrender his watch to the restless and gesticulating marauder. This hint sufficed for my remaining senses, and having wheeled about, I began to make the best of my way to the main road about 100 yards distant, and never did I run faster in all my life. The Prussian observing this, came at full speed after me, and so near had he approached that I every moment expected to receive the contents of his carbine or pistols.

Happily the fear of exciting alarm prevented this result, and I had just put my foot upon the hard road (and no shipwrecked mariner ever rejoiced more to land on a rock of safety) when my pursuer turned his horse's head in another direction, seemingly towards the road to Nivelles, where I doubt not he had left some escort, to skirmish over the field of battle, and plunder its visitors.

Captain C, in the meantime, had with difficulty overtaken our clumsy vehicle, which, slow as it moved, had nevertheless advanced beyond the parallel of our manoeuvres, which our coachman no more expected than ourselves had caused us to rejoin him from the rear instead of from the front. We soon resumed our seats, and poor Mr. M. looked very pale for some time after he had received our congratulations on his escape. Well he might; for it seems that on approaching him the Prussian uttered an exclamation so like "*tombez,*" that Mr. M., taking him at his word (to which the action of the sabre seemed so suitable) "*tombeyed* flat as a flounder," and would fain have laid there quietly, but that the Prussian made his vile jargon too intelligible, by touching Mr. M. with the point of his sword until he got upon one knee, then on his feet, and after, on receiving a *pointed hint* that his watch was wanted, he surrendered this article, and, in fact, completed those manoeuvres which I before described as being the telegraphic despatches that I so fortunately understood in time to make a most masterly retreat.

Mr. M. told us that the Prussian (like a *cossack*, as perhaps he was) first put the watch to his ear, and then into a pocket, where it seemed to jingle among others either found or stolen before he met us. Our terrified companion, however, received no personal injury, and treated the loss of twenty guineas (the value of his watch, chain, and seals), very philosophically. "I remember," he added, "that the fellow's helmet, *moustachios*, whiskers, and accoutrements, so concealed his real features, that even were there a chance of seeing him again, he (Mr. M.) would have been reluctant to identify the man on oath; though perhaps he might recognize his discordant voice and fiendlike eye."

On reaching *La Haye Sainte* again, the carriage stopped for a few minutes, while Captain C. and myself took a farewell view of this interesting spot; Mr. M.'s eagerness for sights being somewhat abated, he declined quitting the vehicle, and soon had the laugh against us, for while conversing with a poor wounded Frenchman, who, as he leaned against the walk, told us "the musket balls were still flying about his head," we were suddenly convinced this was not the effect of delirium, by hearing one whiz over Captain C.'s head, and not very far from mine. Whence it came, however, we were unable to discover, unless from some stragglers who lay secreted behind the opposite hedges, and who were wantonly firing off the muskets they found lying about. On the shot being fired we took the hint, quitted the dangerous spot, and happily got back to the little inn at Waterloo about five p.m. without any further molestation.

We here found two poor Belgians quite ready to sympathize in the effects of so many hair-breadth escapes upon our minds; for it seems that they (who had actually visited the field of slaughter for the purpose of administering relief to the sufferers), were not exempt from the robbery of some fellow in a Prussian uniform (I will not, for the honour of old Blucher and his brave compatriots, say Prussian *soldier*,) who had taken away their own money, and the provisions they carried for the wounded.

Thus was the basest inhumanity added to theft, by a wretch of whom the benevolent Belgians gave a description that convinced Mr. M. it must have been the same who so promptly relieved him of his watch. We therefore regretted more than ever the impossibility of punishing such iniquity. There were too many other matters, however, to occupy the attention of those who had the legal or physical powers to be serviceable, for us to think even of seeking redress through them, so we solaced our brother sufferers in a bottle of good Burgundy, which had been left as a *corps de reserve* in the back of the carriage, and once more drank success to the Allies.

While thus seated at the door of the little inn before mentioned, we heard various accounts of the late "affair," as it was carelessly termed. Some said that from east to west the field of battle did not extend beyond three or four miles, and therefore it was rendered so bloody. Others spoke of the numbers being on the part of the French 100,000 men, containing a great majority of cavalry over the Allied Forces, only 60,000 of whom could be brought into action on the 18th of June, so great were their losses on the 16th, and so impossible had it become for the Duke of Wellington to assemble all the troops under his command in Belgium.

Now, although I do not vouch for the authenticity of these reports, I confess they were not sufficiently shaken by any subsequent inquiries at Brussels to make me alter these memoranda, made on the spot. After, therefore, failing to obtain (without violating decorum) a sight of Lord Uxbridge, whom we were told lay here, and was about to undergo, or had undergone, the amputation of his leg, we once more renewed our route.

The gloomy road to Brussels, through the wood of Soignes, was now rendered more dismal by the approach of night, and it was almost as impassable as in the morning, from the increased number of broken carriages, dead horses, and even human bodies, which lay on each side of us. While, therefore, cautiously pursuing our way, and occupied with deep and sad reflections on the scenes we had witnessed, our attention was suddenly roused by seeing two fierce-looking fellows ride up to the coach door, and desire our driver instantly to stop. Their language was French, and their military dress unlike any we had seen throughout the day.

It is not to be wondered at, therefore, if, under existing circumstances, we took them for thieves, robbers, and marauders! A few civil words, however, from the better dressed one having in some degree restored our composure, we were rejoiced to find them only *gens d'armes,* employed by the Belgic government to prevent plunderers from carrying anything from the field of battle. Inasmuch, therefore, as I had actually brought off a very beautiful *cuirass,* we *were* amenable to this flattering denomination, and readily yielded our prize when we found they wanted nothing more. So, after the exchange of their apologies and our thanks for so much *politesse* (each no doubt uttered with equal sincerity), they rode off for Waterloo, and we once more jogged on towards Brussels, almost doubting if we should ever get there in safety.

Happily we did, and I was rejoiced to think that these *gens d'armes* (if such they really were) had left us the captured newspapers, letters, handkerchiefs, and silk stockings: articles, after all, far more portable, and perhaps more valuable than the heavy *cuirass,* whereof so many could afterwards be bought for a few *francs* at that time.

We found several wounded guests added to the number of those we had left at our hotel in the morning, and were

52

happy to amuse them by a detail of the preceding adventures. In return, they related various anecdotes respecting the battle and its heroes, of which, as far as my memory permitted, I noted down the following:—

An officer, being asked whether he was at the Duchess of Richmond's ball in Brussels on the 16th of June, said, 'No; but I had the good fortune to be at Buonaparte's *rout* on the 18th, at Waterloo!

General Byng, we heard, had many narrow escapes, and among others, one from a ball which, perforating his cloak, passed between his arm and his side.

A foreign regiment of cavalry (I believe some Belgian Hussars), being desired by the Duke of Wellington to keep under the brow of a hill, because, as raw troops, they might not be used till actually wanted, their Colonel (who it seems was afterwards brought to a court martial by his own soldiers), immediately thanked the commander-in-chief for such consideration, and soon after seconded it by leading his troops away from the approach of the enemy to Brussels as hard as they could gallop. This, I suspect, was the cause of the first alarm felt by the inhabitants.

Shaw, the pugilist, who was in the Horse Guards, is said to have dealt destruction around him by the power of his arm; and a comrade related that he saw our English Hercules cut right through the helmet of a cuirassier, whose face was actually divided by the blow!

Col. Kelly, of the Guards, was also reported to have entered into single combat with a colonel of the Imperial Guard, to have vanquished him, and brought off the Frenchman's epaulettes and sword as trophies of his victory!

June 23.—During this day we were chiefly occupied in making preparations to rejoin our little barque at Ostend, and to return to England. I happened, however, in the course of the morning, to meet with two of my countrymen and acquaintances who were about to return by a route which they said would occupy very little more time, while it gratified my ardent desire to have a peep at Holland. Instead, therefore, of accompanying my former comrades, Capt. C. and Mr. M., to Ghent again, I took out a passport, and set off the following morning with Messrs. T. and S., for Antwerp, *alias* Anvers. The distance is about 25 miles, and the charge of 50 *francs* we thought rather exorbitant, but these were times in which cabriolets continued in great request.

We passed through the town of Malines, so famous for its cathedral, and manufacture of lace; we dared not, however, stay to view either, for fear of being shut out of Antwerp, the gates of which were closed at nine, and it wanted but a quarter to nine when we arrived. We found good accommodation at the sign of L'Ours; and having enjoyed our comfortable beds till a late hour the next morning, we were obliged to fag harder during the rest of this day, which was all the time we could spare for viewing the numerous sights of such a far-famed city. Antwerp, while its fortifications are preserved, will ever be important. It will also be long celebrated as the birthplace of Vandyke, while its lofty tower, the height of which is 400 feet, renders it exceedingly conspicuous. Here, as in Brussels, many of our poor wounded countrymen appeared hobbling or lying about the streets, for most of the houses and hospitals (many of which we visited) were overflowing with patients.

However, I must add that the attention of the inhabitants to those who were out of doors, in a great degree compensated for the hardship, and perhaps while the weather continued fine, they suffered but little in consequence. Be that as it may, every one of these brave fellows seemed so perfectly content with his lot, and so resigned to his fate, as to afford us a great degree of consolation in contemplating them. The majority appeared to be Highlanders, and were probably wounded on the 16th, and were thus far removed that they might the more easily be embarked for England, in case the battle of the 18th had gone against us.

The prisons (we were told) had been filled by French prisoners, but time did not allow us to visit them; and the owner of the celebrated Chapeau de Paille, by Rubens, for some inexplicable reasons, would not allow anyone to visit him this morning. We regretted, therefore, that the time wasted in attempting to do so had not been employed in viewing the prisons. But these are the vicissitudes all travellers must expect. So we contented ourselves with mounting the lofty tower before mentioned, and were amply repaid by the extensive views it affords. In this cathedral is buried the famous blacksmith who became an artist, and obtained the daughter of a painter for his wife. His epitaph or motto is

Connubialis amor, de Mulciebre fecit Apellem.

We viewed the *corderie* or rope walk built by Buonaparte, near the Citadel. It is above 1000 feet long, and was intended to manufacture cables for the men of war that were formerly so numerous in the dock here, although one solitary Dutch vessel of war now only remained. The great and perhaps unrivalled street (for length or breadth) which adorns Antwerp, needs no description here; but, combined with the advantages of a river (the Scheldt), which admits of the largest vessels coming up almost to the very quay; fortifications comparatively impregnable, and a tower almost incomparable, it must be allowed that this city has not been celebrated without just cause. The houses, too, are lofty, and built much in the old Spanish style.

Before I leave Antwerp I would mention that the church of Notre Dame contains some beautiful paintings, among the most conspicuous of which are Christ's Descent, and the Lord's Supper, both by Rubens. There are also several full-length figures of the Evangelists, superbly chiselled, together with a monument of Marcus Antoninus, who appears in robes that require you almost to touch them before you can be satisfied they are of marble. The clock, too, which is on a globe that goes round and displays the hour on its face, was to me an object of novelty and curiosity.

It is said that the Exchange here was the model from which Sir Thomas Gresham built that in London. Indeed the city of Antwerp formerly excited so much admiration, that Charles the Fifth said it ought to be kept in a glass case, and shewn only once a year !

Early in the morning of the 25th we took our departure from Antwerp in a vehicle like a curricle, with this difference only—that it carried three, that the postillion rode on one of the horses, and that the pole was supported by a bar below their bellies instead of over their backs, as in England.

At the first inn we reached in Holland, they made us sensible of our disadvantageous change in point of expense, since for what we regularly paid a *franc* (l0d.) in Belgium, we were here charged a florin (20d.) We experienced the same difference all through Holland, with much less comfort for our money. The roads, too, were worse, and nine hours had expired before we reached Mardyke, a distance of about thirty miles, and the coachman's charge was fifty francs. Here it was necessary to cross a piece of water, about two miles broad, called Holland Diep, for which we paid two florins; and having hired a sort of hack chariot on the other side for a Napoleon, we proceeded six miles further to another ferry, and were again rowed across a *diep*, for which, besides the fare, we were charged half a florin each for stepping on the quay at the opposite side.

Indeed, so regularly did they exact a payment for every movement, that my comrade observed, he wondered they had not charged something extra for the fair wind that favoured us, which would have appeared not less imposing. In saying this, perhaps he was somewhat influenced by the warning given him by a veteran traveller at Antwerp, who said, "Remember, the moment you enter Holland, to pay only half what they ask you." This, however, could only apply to purchases, and not to travelling expenses, for on refusing to pay some of their exorbitant demands, the Dutch boors refused to let us advance. At a lone inn, therefore, without any tribunal to apply to for redress, what was our remedy?

For my part, I had seen so much more difficulty created by an endeavour to lessen the charges (while travelling in Spain under similar circumstances) that I persisted in subduing the John Bull indignation of my comrade, who, understanding a little Dutch, was paymaster; so we all sat down to a large piece of boiled veal (the prevailing dish hereabouts), and drank our Geneva, under a full impression that in future we had better submit a little more than make enemies of those on whom we were so dependent—

Levus fit patientia quicquid corrigere est nefas.

Rotterdam.—It was late in the evening before we reached Rotterdam, which we did in safety after crossing the Maes (river), but were obliged to *pay* for having the gates open to us at such an hour. A porter, or I should more properly say a Dutch boor, next assailed (not petitioned) us for permission to carry our luggage to the hotel called the Bath House. It was with difficulty, however, we could satisfy the fellow with less than five florins (seven shillings), which was an exorbitant demand for wheeling a barrow the distance of a quarter of a mile. Nor did the waiter dare to acknowledge (till the impostor was gone) that *half* the money would have exceeded his due.

The inn being furnished with baths (whence its name),

I was greatly refreshed by one of those luxuries after the damp and chilling journey we had had, through a country as uninteresting as swamps could make it. We had a good supper and tolerable beds. The next morning, daylight came sneaking into my heavy-framed window, through the trees, which here, and throughout the whole town were regularly planted within a few feet of the houses, and made me anticipate that the rays of the sun were like those of a tropical clime—too powerful to be endured without these rural blinds. Greatly, however, was I disappointed, for they were even more languid than in England, while the canals, which, as well as the Maes, intersect this city in all directions, made us imagine everything to be damp about it.

We allowed the day to be far advanced before we sallied forth "in quest of sights;" and finding that the Exchange began to fill about one o'clock, we bent our steps towards this most important edifice in or to Rotterdam, "whose soul is commerce." After being pushed about by people of all nations, in a place too much like the late Exchange at London both in size and shape to require comment or description, we came out full of political rumours. These we soon exchanged for clouds of smoke, which it was impossible to avoid inhaling, in a neighbouring coffeehouse, where my companions had occasion to seek a Dutch friend, and who was so enveloped in it that we had great difficulty in finding him. I regretted having exhausted all my cigars, which in such a place would have proved so excellent a defence. To avoid being choked, however, we were obliged to pledge our new Holland acquaintance in a glass of pure Schiedam—followed by an English d—n too.

The next thing we saw was the statue of Erasmus, who, if his genius was at all in proportion to the height of this figure, which is at least six feet three inches, must have been a wonderful Dutchman indeed, even in those times. Happily, however, there remain some better proofs of his exaltation than this; and over the little obscure place where he was born is inscribed—

Ædibus his ortus, mundum decoravit Erasmus,
Artibus ingenius, religione, fide.

Being represented in the figure with his fur gown and cap (the habit of Doctor), and holding a book in one hand, while turning a leaf with the other, the children say he turns it over directly he *hears* the clock strike one—and men believe them!

Few places, I should imagine, could be more favourably situated for mercantile pursuits than Rotterdam; for, independent of the innumerable canals throughout the streets, it is only about five leagues distant from Helvoetsluys, with which, and the main ocean, the communication is easy. The Maes, too, being joined by the Rhine, causes a very considerable influx of commerce to flow from Germany to.

Rotterdam. Vessels of 800 tons and upwards come down this latter river, which besides being deeply laden with goods, have actually suites of apartments fitted up for passengers, who are continually descending the Rhine on their way through Holland, or to embark at Helvoetsluys for England. Immense shoals of timber also come by this same channel from the north to Rotterdam, whence they are afterwards shipped to all parts of Europe.

The various canals which in open weather are sources of profit and convenience to the Dutch, become in winter very beneficial in preserving the health and diverting the minds of the inhabitants. Persons of all ranks and both sexes are during frost seen displaying their agility on the slippery surface of the ice; and even carriages pass safely across the frozen mass.

We hired a sort of hackney coach to take us to the Hague, a distance of twelve miles, and in our way passed through the famous city of Delft, which, although only six miles from Rotterdam, was a resting place for our driver, and happily, for us, since it afforded the opportunity, upon which we hardly calculated, of seeing the city, and admiring its two beautiful streets. It is from this port that Leyden and the Hague draw their chief supplies of coals, corn, wine, &c. It is the landing place of foreign ambassadors, and is celebrated as the birthplace of Grotius. The principal magazine of powder and armoury was formerly kept here, and the manufacture of their best kind of porcelain ware. It is not generally known, however, that this was ruined by the immense importations of real china made by the Dutch East India Company, who could afford to sell that at a lower rate than the almost equally beautiful fabric of their own country, which is consequently falling into disuse.

The church is very beautiful, the country tolerably verdant, and the town apparently surrounded by a dyke, but it being dusk we pushed on to the Hague, a distance of five miles further. This we accomplished in time to obtain a most excellent supper at an inn called the Marechal de Turenne, which was kept by a man named *Handel,* who certainly did accommodate us to one of the best tunes we had heard in Holland, *viz.*, the "roast beef of Old England."

At seven o'clock the following morning we walked as far as a little fishing place called Scheveling, about two miles distant, not less renowned for its herrings than reverenced as the port at which the Nassau family first landed in Holland on their return from England. The King of the Netherlands, as an encouragement to the fisheries, annually presents a silver herring to the first fisherman who produces one alive after the season has commenced.

We returned through the beautiful grounds attached to the Palace of the Queen Dowager, also about two miles from the Hague, and were particularly struck by the neatness and order, divested of the usual Dutch formality, which prevailed throughout these elegant gardens and luxuriant woods. The house is embosomed among them, but being then fully occupied by the Dowager's establishment, was not open to the public. Happily the *Marechal de Turenne was,* and thither we arrived about eleven, half famished, and tolerably fagged by our ramble. Of what Mr. Handel provided for breakfast, and still less of what we ate, I should be ashamed to write lest we be taken for gourmands. Suffice it to say, that no inn in Scotland ever produced a better dejeuner, nor did any Scotchmen ever do greater justice to such a bountiful repast.

Of the Hague, indeed, so much might be said and written as would fill my memorandum book: but so much *has* already been written on the subject, that it would be presumptuous on my part to add more than that *I* thought His Majesty's chief residence here very large and very comfortable, if not quite so superb as the palaces of France and Spain. By the way, the Ambassador from the latter country is the *only* one who does, or did till very lately, reside in a house belonging to and built by the Spanish government for their representative at this court. The other foreign ministers, however, are not uncomfortably lodged in buildings something like those which surround Grosvenor-square, having large plate-glass windows, and altogether stately fronts.

The young Prince of Orange had been strongly invited by the Royal Family to come hither after being wounded at Waterloo; but it seems that his Royal Highness had more confidence in some of the English surgeons at Brussels, who very properly advised him not to move about unnecessarily in such a state to any part.

The Hague is certainly well adapted for a brilliant Court, from the number of its squares, the style of the houses, and the great variety of pleasant rides by which it is surrounded. Nor was this city ill chosen by the King of the Netherlands for his present residence, being at an accessible distance from the seat of war and Brussels, besides being so near the sea as would, in case of emergency, have permitted the Royal Family to embark for England or elsewhere at a short notice. We found the inhabitants of the Hague (as was very natural, of course, from their more frequent intercourse with foreigners), speaking almost every European language; and while it relieved us greatly from the dumb show we had been obliged to practice so much since our arrival in Holland, it added to the many prepossessions we felt in favour of the Hague, a city we reluctantly quitted.

The theatre was represented to us as a very good one, but we had no opportunity of seeing the interior. This place, however, not being so much the residence of Buonaparte's brother, Louis (while King of Holland) as Amsterdam, the public amusements once so numerous here had been little encouraged then; and the restored Monarch had but little spare cash wherewith to economize them now. I saw no sedan chairs in this place, but several hackney coaches on a stand as at Brussels.

June 28.—Early this morning we took our departure in a *Treck sckuyt* for Leyden. It starts and arrives with the punctuality of an English mail, although it only moves with half the speed; and its readiness to be off is announced by the ringing of a little bell instead of a long horn. In a Catholic country you might suppose this bell to indicate the approach of a sacred procession. The banks of the canal presented the usual sameness of this flat country, until we approached Leyden—a distance of five leagues, which we accomplished in four hours !

Just as we were landing, a large plot of ground on the bank of the canal was pointed out to us as having been suddenly rendered bare some few years since by the explosion of a barge containing 40,000 lbs. weight of gunpowder, that Buonaparte was sending to Antwerp. The shock must, indeed, have been as terrific as it was instantaneous, having uncovered at a blow more than an acre of ground.

We were conducted to the Lion d'Or, where, finding the *table d'hôte* ready, we took our station among twenty more guests, and fared but indifferently. The inn, however, is by no means a very bad one, but then overflowing with visitors, it was less comfortable than usual. Being informed that there was little chance of securing good beds, we resolved to take a hasty survey of this celebrated seat of learning, and proceed on our journey, or perhaps I should more properly say, our *voyage,* in time to reach some excellent quarters at Haerlem that night.

Leyden is a large and certainly a beautiful city, and, although fortified, is, like Ostend, protected by the power of laying all the surrounding country under water in case of an enemy's approach. This, indeed, the citizens did, by the advice of the Prince of Orange, when they were besieged by the Spaniards in 1574. Then nearly 2000 of the latter were drowned! The besieged were, nevertheless, reduced to great straits, as is shewn by a picture in the *Stadthouse,* representing a citizen in the act of gnawing one arm while fighting with the other. There is also another curious picture, which is said to be the oldest in Holland, shewn at the same place. Its antiquity is in some degree proved by the faded colours of its singular figures, which are surrounded by a frame dividing the painting into three parts, the two sides or wings thereof being on hinges, that shut in upon the picture, and preserve it from general view—a very good plan, adopted at the time of the Reformation of 1380.

The subject of the picture is the Crucifixion of our Saviour. On the opposite side of the room is a representation of the Infernal regions, by Buke, of Leyden (I think), well adapted to intimidate sinners by its horrors. Another good painting presents portraits of the burgomasters (singularly habited in Spanish dresses), consulting for the defence of their city when besieged by the Duke of Alva.

As we were quitting the *Stadthouse* our attention was attracted by a very interesting young man and woman, who, accompanied by their parents and friends, were swearing fidelity to each other before a magistrate—a ceremony whereby they were married. We were informed that it had been established by Napoleon, and still prevailed in most parts of Holland.

In passing along the street to the Botanical Garden, we observed the name of Murray over a bookseller's shop, and were tempted to inquire if it really was kept by a countryman of ours. We paid dearly, however, for the gratification of this curiosity in the price of a few books that we bought there. They were chiefly French comedies, unbound. Murray informed us, that when the University was in a state of prosperity, his father had been encouraged to establish that shop which the present possessor (who, though born in Holland, still retained the traits of Caledonian lineage), obtained by inheritance. He is, I should think, 70 years of age.

The Botanical Gardens afforded us very considerable gratification, from the manner in which they are laid out, and the immense number of rare plants wherewith they abound. Nor is the adjoining Museum less deserving of attention, being stored with specimens from all parts of the world, and particularly with those of anatomy. Among the latter they show you the singularly diminutive foetus of a child, whose features appear to be as well formed, and in fact exactly resemble those of a man of 90 years of age.

The students of the University are now so few as hardly to deserve notice, and in fact it has been gradually degenerating of late years. Dr. Boerhaave was one of the luminaries who formerly shone at this University, and many English noblemen have been educated here, as well as German and French *savans*. It was founded so long since as 1575, as a reward to the inhabitants for so nobly withstanding the tremendous siege of the Spaniards, under the Duke of Alva.

The old and new canals of the Rhine here form a sort of angle, where there are said to be some remains of an ancient Saxon castle that we could not spare time to see. By means of these accommodating *Treck sckuyts*, therefore, we were able to reach Haerlem that evening in four hours. The country on both sides was flat and dreary. The great Lake of Haerlem, however, which we saw on our left, deserves notice. It seemed to lie between Leyden, Haerlem, and Amsterdam, and is said to be at least twelve or fourteen miles long, and nearly as broad; abounding with fish, particularly eels, of an immense size. When Haerlem was besieged by the Spaniards, the fleet of the latter engaged that of the Dutch upon its surface. The neighbouring slough affords a considerable supply of turf for fuel to nearly 400,000 inhabitants.

We were again lodged at a "Lion d'Or," (kept by one Godthart), at Haerlem, whose two pretty little daughters came out to welcome us to their inn. After an indifferent dinner and a long voyage, we were indeed most agreeably surprised to have for supper as good a beef steak as ever I tasted in England, supported by two dishes of excellent green peas, which were followed by some Burgundy, equally deserving of praise. We then retired early to enjoy the nice clean beds these little maidens had so carefully prepared for us; and were so refreshed by these comforts as to be able to commence our ramble through Haerlem early the next morning.

The first thing which struck us in going out of the inn door was a child's cap hanging over the next door, (to denote an *accouchement* within), a fashion we learned that had existed since the Spaniards took this place, when they had sufficient gallantry to allow such a symbol on all occasions, to preserve the house from the rude obtrusions of the soldiery— warning the inhabitants, however, as they valued this privilege, never to abuse it.

Our guide next pointed out the House in which Coster, the inventor of printing, is said to have been born: a habitation that, like that of Shakespeare, in Stratford, would have otherwise been too insignificant to notice.

After seeing the great church, and paying eleven florins to the organist for playing the Battle of Prague, and finely imitating a storm upon this organ (so well known for its incomparable magnitude and tones, and for having cost one and a half ton of gold to build, possessing 5000 pipes, the largest of which is 38 feet long), we were reluctantly hurried away to see a neighbouring fair that had begun today, and was to last several weeks, in the park of a palace now inhabited by the Royal Family, but formerly belonging to the celebrated and opulent Mr. Hope. The style of the building is evidently English, and it is ornamented with some beautiful sculpture.

Some of the Princes being there, etiquette forbade our admission, but this was done in so polite a manner, as greatly to diminish our disappointment. Nothing surely can be more cheerful than the appearance of a Dutch fair; exceeding, of course, in abundance of toys, and certainly in diversity of amusements, any I ever saw in England. All kinds of rustic games were performed by the heavy Dutch on this occasion in a manner that made us think ourselves in France or Italy.

The booths and shows, too, were ranged with a formality, that, although very like those of England, manifested a superiority which made us think we owe these festivals, as well as much of our language, to Holland. I will endeavour to give proof of this by the few following examples:—

Dutch.—De wind was goodt.
English.—The wind was good.
Dutch.—Glasse o' goodt wyn, brandy wyn, beer.

English.—Glass of good wine, brandy, beer.

Dutch.—Wy eet een salaad, greene herbe, apples ende peeres. .

English.—We ate a salad, green herbs, apples and pears.

Dutch.—Vis, fles, white brood ende buter.

English.—Fish, flesh, white bread and butter.

Dutch.—Achter all come de tee, coffee, chocolade.

English.—After all came the tea, coffee, and chocolate.

Cum multis aliis.

I cannot, however, quit this delightful fair without noticing a particular class of men there whom we observed to be always going at a sort of jog trot, but never walking; we were informed they belonged to a neighbouring village famous for this active race, and celebrated for the long and rapid journeys they were thus able to perform. On returning to the town we passed some alms-houses, erected by an English merchant named Taylor, who realized a fortune here, which he left to the inhabitants. Besides the above charitable institution, we were shewn the Public Museum, containing a superb collection of minerals, an enormous electrifying machine, and various optical glasses by Dollond, Adams, &c.

A magnificent library is attached, and for keeping the whole in repair Mr. Taylor left eight millions of florins, the interest of which should be devoted to that purpose by four of the principal inhabitants of Haerlem, or for making acquisitions to this already valuable store. This place, therefore, had much to gratify the feelings of an Englishman, and we were almost sorry to be obliged to proceed at night to Amsterdam, a distance of eight or ten miles, which occupied two hours, and we passed several gentlemen's gardens on the banks of the canal which fully proved the favourable nature of this soil for flowers, particularly tulips, of which large quantities of roots are being annually exported from Haerlem and Leyden. We went to the sign of the Amsterdam Arms, that, like the inn at Rotterdam, was large and dirty; and were shewn into the public room to supper, but found no beefsteaks or green peas there, nor anything good enough to mention.

This city takes its name from the River Amstel (of which it may be called, as their great square is, the Dam); it was built on piles, chiefly of fir, driven perpendicularly into the ground. These caused Erasmus facetiously to describe it as a place "where the inhabitants lived on the tops of trees." Indeed, when one hears that 6,000 piles were required to support one steeple, and that the foundation of the *Stadt-house* cost £100,000 for timber, we must allow the justice of the philosopher's remark. That building, which cost altogether £3,000,000 sterling, deserves very particular attention also for the superstructure, which, though rather heavy, is truly substantial and magnificent. On its summit is an immense Atlas of brass, bearing on his shoulders a copper globe, larger than that of St. Peter's at Rome.

In front of this edifice is 110 paces, and inside and out appears to be incrusted with marble. It has a beautiful bas relief, several fine statues, and pillars of the Corinthian order. The ball room appeared to be about 70 feet high, 60 broad, and 120 long, and over the Secretary's Chamber was the very emblematical figure of fidelity—a dog pining beside the corpse of its master. Not far distant (what a mixture!) is the gloomy hall which is reserved for passing sentence on condemned criminals, surrounded by allegorical bas reliefs, while in another part of the building is a very extensive museum, always gratuitously open to the public, and grateful ought they to be for this privilege. It contains some exquisite paintings by the first masters, which I believe were preserved by Louis Buonaparte from the rude hands of his brother soldiers.

For one choice picture by Van Helet (his reputed masterpiece), which represent a celebration of "the Siege of Munster," by the principal officers of Amsterdam, and contains portraits of each), the Dutch tell you three tons and a half of gold has been refused, but they do not state by whom that sum was offered! Sir Joshua Reynolds is also said to have admired it exceedingly. "The Night Watch," by Rembrandt, is excellent; but the little *bijou* of all their collection seemed to be a small picture of a "School by Night," by Gerard Dow, wherein the five different grades of shadow are so beautifully executed as to attract the attention of the most superficial observer. This gem is kept in a case, and is said to have been taken out of a vessel captured from the French. It is valued at 15,000 florins, and was supposed to be intended as a present from some grandee of Russia to Napoleon.

We next saw Van Tromp's armour, which is more to be admired for its weight than its elegance. On the floor were inlaid two enormous globes—the celestial and terrestrial—and in the window was a curious old clock, made entirely of bones instead of wood or metal. To crown, or I should more properly say to support, the whole, the very vaults of this stupendous building are adopted for the great and wealthy Bank of Amsterdam.

Not far off is the Exchange, which is larger than that of Antweip, but not so handsome as that of London.

The streets are wide, though often intersected by canals; Churches and Hospitals were also numerous. Religions of every kind seem to be tolerated here, and no where do the Jews experience more indulgence. When Louis the Eighteenth is said to have so far admitted them to the rights of citizens on payment of taxes, &c, they settled themselves through this city, with the adopted names of flowers, fruits, birds, and beasts, but not of towns or villages, that being forbidden; why, I could never learn, though I suspect for political reasons. Their synagogues, as in England, produce some of the finest singers.

As we were rambling about the town, after dinner, a blaze of light from a sort of saloon attracted us to the door, which for a florin each the porter said we might enter. We did so, and soon discovered it to be a sort of Vauxhall called a "*rondel.*" At a Dutch *Rondel*, the master or mistress presides at a bar, and music is playing in the centre of the shabby saloon, which being surrounded, like an English tea garden, with seats, the intermediate space serves as a circle, wherein the company, chiefly consisting of the dissolute, continue to parade.

If among them any fair cyprian effects a conquest, the enamoured swain confesses it by offering her *en passant* a glass of liqueur, which, if she accepts (and rarely did we see it refused), one of the presiding deities is summoned to sanction for a bribe the disposition to favour the solicitations of her new admirer. The latter class were chiefly foreigners, thus confirming what we had previously heard— that few Dutch merchants, however young, however rich, or however gay, would be found here sacrificing at the altar of Venus any of that gold for which they seem to be ever praying at the shrine of Plutus.

Indeed, I understood they seldom quitted their counting houses till a late hour, although they went to them at an early one. Many of the poor girls were so very delicate and lovely, that if the absence of their young countrymen had been caused by purer motives than I suspect, they would surely make some efforts to suppress some of the very many houses of this kind which are to be found in Holland, where the fair sex seem to be more humiliated than in any civilized place I have yet visited. The Dutch burghers, however, on the contrary, take their wives and daughters there, on purpose (as they say) to disgust them with such scenes of vice, dissipation, and extravagance, but thus they sanction it; and I have dwelt longer upon these strange paradoxes in hopes some others may be able to solve them, for I cannot.

Just as we were quitting Amsterdam we learned that there was a curious machine invented for lifting their own heavy ships over a sandbank, which being at the mouth of the river, becomes the great protection of this port against a foreign fleet. It consists of a raft, resembling the two halves (stem and stern) of a flat-bottomed boat, that are made to meet under the keel of a ship, when the former being pumped dry it draws less water than the latter, and thus bears its tremendous burthen safely over this impediment of nature.

The forts, however, of Naarden and the Helder, (if they were stored sufficiently) it is said would resist a siege of two years, and protect more efficaciously the entrance to the Zuyder Zee than the above sandbank, that might perhaps be passed by boats.

Amsterdam, I should add, is supplied with fresh water by the Rhine, whose ancient course was diverted from Leyden towards this more populous and thriving city.

Those who have visited the neighbouring villages of Sardan and Brock will, I think, sympathize in the regret we experienced at being unable to do so. The former is famed as the place wherein the Emperor Peter of Russia learned the art of ship-building, in the disguise of a common workman; and the latter for the peculiarly antique dress of its inhabitants, their extreme cleanliness, and their Chinese-like habitations. But we were obliged to set off for Utrecht early this morning, and, embarking in a *sckuyt* on the Amstel, we passed I believe into another river, called the Val, and afterwards pursued our voyage along a canal, accomplishing in eight hours a distance of thirty miles.

The time, nevertheless, did not appear tedious, as the banks on both sides were ornamented with gardens belonging to country seats, most of them having at the water's edge a summer-house wherein the Dutch were enjoying their pipes, and in front of which there was some odd inscription, such as—"This is my dear retreat;" "My blessing;" "A Dutchman's real joy;" "Love of trees;" "Happy hours;" "Our dear retreat;" &c.

We drove to the Castle of Antwerp Hotel, and rising first in the morning, I saw from my window the Church of Utrecht, which is 1100 years old, and its tower with 446 stairs. It presents a singular appearance, a portion of it having been destroyed by a storm some years since. It still remains in this dilapidated state, a monument of the poverty or indolence of the people.

After a breakfast worthy of Scotland or the Hague, we accepted the offer of a guide who spoke both French and English well, to show us the lions of this ancient city, which, standing about fifty feet above the level of the sea, and possessing an excellent habitation for a King, besides its literary resources, was naturally, and I think wisely, selected by Louis Buonaparte as a favourite residence. His wife, however, preferred the gayer circle of Paris, in which she could move so conspicuously under the patronage of Napoleon, and she was generally there.

Utrecht will ever be memorable for the union of the seven provinces having been first arranged there, and the subsequent well-known treaty of 1662, which bears its name. The room in the *Stadthouse* wherein it was signed is shewn to visitors. Of the University once so celebrated, alas! but little can now be said. A few students appeared wandering about the streets or through the groves and cloisters, which still bespeak this place to have been long the a resort of the most polished Dutch, and their proudest seat of learning.

At all events, it rivalled Leyden in the former, if not in the latter respect; as, owing to the want of such valuable botanical gardens, the science of physic is less pursued at

Utrecht than astronomy and divinity.

The soil in the neighbourhood is light and good; living is cheap, and I am told, that not many years ago the students were lodged and boarded for a dollar per week! (say 5s.) Perhaps a few florins more would suffice at present; if so, some of our young gentlemen at Oxford and Cambridge might save a fortune, and possibly gain as much learning by "going to college" abroad for a few years here, as many of our young noblesse were wont to do formerly. Altogether there are now only sixty students at this University!

Before quitting Utrecht it seemed so indispensable to visit the neighbouring village of Zelst, about nine miles distant, that we resolved to devote the next morning to the purpose, and, as our guide foretold, we never repented this resolve, for not only was the road thither good, and the day fine, but the country through which we passed both verdant and romantic.

We stopped on our way at a small but neat little village, bearing the no less romantic name of "Rosenberg," which is in the centre of an extensive property, lately bought by a rich and ambitious Dutchman, for the sole purpose of acquiring the high-sounding title of Lord of Rosenberg!

Buried in one of the thick woods wherewith this fine estate abounds, we were guided to the cave of an Anchorite named Le Brun, who, during the French Revolution, sought and found that refuge here from whence he had but very lately been taken by the hand of Death! The poor old man had prepared the grave wherein he now lay, not far distant from the cell he had so long previously inhabited. Missing him about their hamlet, the simple villagers were some days ere they suspected that the old hermit had paid the debt of nature. At length they sought and found his withered corpse stretched near the place so long marked for its reception. Placing, therefore, a sod over the grave, some friendly Druid is said to have added the board which

73

bears this almost obliterated inscription:—

In pace obiit Frater Hildebrandus
Die calendis Martius anno 1808.
MEMENTO MORI..

To him succeeded the present tenant of this dreary abode—a venerable man of 80 years of age, whose grey beard reaching to his waist, encircled by a cord, and clothed in the coarsest garb of a Capuchin, gave to his appearance little less interest than the memory of his predecessor. We knew, however, that the former had been expatriated by the horrors of anarchy, and had been forced to change a life of luxury for a hermit's cell as the price of his existence. The latter I suspected to be a pauper, who was encouraged by the ostentatious "Lord of Rosenberg" to play this part, and ornament a spot too often visited now to be dismal in itself or unproductive to its occupier.

We laid a few florins on the leaves of a bible, which, with a skull, covered entirely the rustic table. We smiled at the formal bed of rushes, and quitted the forest after reading, at our hermit's request, the following passages on the walls of his residence (translated from the Dutch by our guide), "God preserve this man in his old age, and may each visitor give him that which he cannot ask for !

SOLIUS SOLITUDINE.
Over the door is written
Artica via est quæ ducit ad vitam.

While putting down our names in the register this venerable man keeps of those who visit him, he said the present "Lord of Rosenberg" had offered to build him a more substantial cave near his own palace, to which we now bent our steps; but hearing that we had no chance of admittance, and seeing a steep hill in the way, we rejoined our carriage, and proceeded to the village of Zelst, where we found a very excellent hotel, and were furnished with a repast called a breakfast, consisting of strawberries, cherries, eggs, ham, tea, coffee, and rolls of exquisite sweetness, for which (I must record ere it escape me) we paid only one florin each, and ultimately left our landlord as satisfied with this as was the attendant at the unexpected donation of a *sous* from every guest.

We proceeded, therefore, in very good humour, to visit the little colony of Moravians who are settled here, and who form the great attraction of the place. To the interior of a tolerably extensive range of buildings (forming a square) do these interesting and industrious people confine themselves. On entering it we passed under an archway, erected by the grateful colony in honour of the visit paid them lately by the Prince of Orange and the Emperor (Alexander) of Russia. On the front is inscribed

Worship the true God;
Honour your king, and love your country.

In one wing of the building is a chapel, having sweet-toned organ, fitted up with silver pipes; and a College for educating 65 of the young members of the fraternity, who all sleep in separate beds in one immense room, and dine together daily in their spacious hall. The other wing is fitted up with small apartments which are let to the different tradesmen of the community, such as silversmiths, turners, toymen, shoemakers, saddlers, glovers, and tinmen, who shewed us many ingenious articles manufactured for sale, on which a price is fixed, and no abatement made.

We bought a few trifles on moderate terms; but what chiefly diverted us was to observe the peculiar colours of the ribbons, which, being placed in the caps of their neat, quaker-like dressed females, distinguished them, as—for the married, blue; for the single, red; for the widow, white. This, we afterwards learned, was practised by other colonies of

Moravians at Ernut and Murat.

We returned very comfortably to Utrecht in the afternoon, and being told we had omitted to see a very curious model of Solomon's Temple (which it was said belonged to a Professor Mail), we hastened to get a glimpse of it, and were fortunate in doing so before dark. It was many years making (they say forty-five!), and occupies a tolerably-sized room in the Professor's house. The doors of it are gilded as well as the pillars, which appeared to be chiefly of the Corinthian and composite orders. The ark, the sacred, and most sacred apartments are also gilded. For the benefit of others I mention that there are inner chambers, wherein we could just perceive the representations of Angels and other attributes of the great Tabernacle; and I regretted the necessity of quitting this curiosity so soon.

Having, however, subtracted one day from the few that the arrangements of my comrades or myself permitted us to devote to Holland, we hurried back from hence to Rotterdam, with a view to embark by the first packet at Helvoetsluys for Harwich, and "the Prince of Orange" was ultimately the one that presented itself for our purpose.

Before I leave Holland altogether, let me observe that although, compared with other countries, there is certainly less to gratify the classic mind, it is far from being void of interest, or deserving the farewell wherewith the sarcastic Voltaire quitted it, to return to the more romantic beauties of France, who said—

Adieu! canards! canaux! canaille!

Nor was our own poet Churchill much less charitable, since, being equally disgusted with the flat appearance of the country, and the phlegmatic temper of the Dutch, his own lively, and perhaps somewhat irritable disposition, indulged in the following strain, in allusion to their dykes and dams: —

Amphibious Dutch! may sudden be your fall!
May man un-dam you, and God d——n you all!

No doubt he was disappointed in finding so few monuments of antiquity in Holland, or such simple churches compared with those of Catholic countries. These very dykes and sluices, however, ought rather to be contemplated as stupendous works of art for the preservation of a country than ridiculed for their abounding. Moreover, too, they exhibit great examples of ingenuity and application, which may safely vie with the more effeminate race who now inhabit the south, and are for the greater part sunk in sloth, voluptuousness, and poverty. It is true there are few amphitheatres, triumphal arches, columns, baths, catacombs, &c, to be found in Holland; but nevertheless there is a neatness and simplicity in many of their buildings which deserve considerable, if not equal, admiration.

In France or Italy the stranger is delighted with works of luxury and fancy, but among the Dutch he must be satisfied to see only those that are of real use and emolument to the public at large.

From Holland we have learned many valuable lessons of commerce and industry, besides reaping other benefits from our constant intercourse with that country; nor should we ever forget the stock from whence so many of our monarchs sprung—the House of Nassau—whose princes, by their wisdom and valour, founded that commonwealth at home which their posterity still inherit and defend. The Belgians and Dutch seem to be a different people, and not likely to agree long together.

Apropos. I remember (as a boy) being at a public dinner, given in London to the King of Holland on his restoration to the throne. Braham, the then celebrated singer, sat opposite me as a guest; and when the public singers engaged sang "God save the King," he (Braham) joined rather loudly. His next neighbour, ignorant of who he was, excited his smile and mine by trying to check him. When, however, the chairman called on Mr. Braham as a favour for a song, the poor man opposite me and next to the great vocalist, was all aghast!

But we are summoned to embark, so I must conclude my hasty journal and go on board, with every sentiment of gratitude to God for having been so preserved through such an interesting and eventful tour.

N. S.

The Particulars of the
Battle of Waterloo

C. W.

Contents

Some Particulars of the Battle of Waterloo   83

Some Particulars of the
Battle of Waterloo

EXTRACTED FROM A LETTER WRITTEN BY SERGEANT C. W. OF THE
THIRD BATTALION, FIRST REGIMENT OF FOOT GUARDS.

Camp, Bois du Bologne, Paris,
29th July, 1815

On the 16th June we marched at four o'clock in the
morning the distance of about twenty-four miles, and then
rushed into action. The Lord gave us great strength, both of
body and mind, on that day and through the whole of our
labours. We arrived just in time, or the enemy would have
forced the Belgians. With one hour and a half's hard fighting we maintained our position with some little advantage,
that our loss was great.

On the 18th of June, the day of Waterloo, we took up
a good position, at the same time leaving the enemy one
they would accept. We opened on the enemy seven guns
before they returned an answer: then most tremendously
the action commenced; but God was with us. I addressed
my company in a few words, to "be steady and attentive
to orders, keep perfect silence, and put your whole trust in
God's help, for he is with us. Be strong and determined; to
use all your skill in levelling; make sure your mark, and in
the charge use all your strength, and you shall see by the
close of day's sun your enemies fly, and the shout of victory

shall be yours."

I felt my mind stayed upon God; and my confidence was so firm, that neither the thunder of our enemy's cannon and musquetry, nor the boast of his guards, nor the threats of his cavalry (in mail), either alarmed my breast or concerned my mind

It was the Sabbath-day; and while you were praying to and praising the King of Glory in his church, I was doing the same in the field of blood: I was truly in the spirit of a Christian and of a soldier on the Lord's day.

The enemy fired round shot and shell, grape and canister, and new horse nails tied up in bundles, nine bundles in a gun: these I saw and handled on the 19th. Unlawful carnage: but the portrait of the man is blood, murder, and desolation.

The third battalion of the First Guards and a battalion of Rifle of the King's German Legion (say 1200 men) advanced 300 paces in front of the whole line into a valley which lay between the two positions, and within 100 yards of about 6000 cavalry and 3000 infantry of the enemy. They viewed us with astonishment; and to prove that God had filled them with fear, they formed square, and neither charged nor fired upon us, except from the height of their position; but we suffered much from these guns: We remained firing at them for half an hour, and then retired into our post in time. The cavalry (in armour) charged us many times in the course of the day, but made no impression: we repulsed them with great slaughter. We never fired at the cavalry till they came within thirty yards.

Towards the evening Bonaparte directed against us his choice 105th regiment; and in half an hour we cut them all to pieces, and took one stand of colours. He then sent us his Grenadier Imperial Guards; they came within 100 yards of us, and ported arms to charge; but we advanced upon them in quick time, and opened a brisk file fire by two ranks. They allowed us to come within about thirty yards of them: they stood till then, looking at us, as if panic-struck, and did not fire:—they then, as we approached, faced about, and fled for their lives in all directions. They did not like the thoughts of the British bayonets, for we had just commenced the charge; they ran very fast, but many of them fell while we pursued, together with one standard of colours; and I have the honour to wear a colonel's sword of the French Imperial Guard.

When the Imperial Guards, the dependence of Bonaparte, ran, his defence departed from him, and his whole line, as has been stated, became confusion. Much to the honour of his grace (as in every case throughout the day), in the space of five minutes, he formed a line in the valley for a general charge, and then the shout of "Victory!" "Victory!" was heard. The very elements rang with voices and cannons on Britain's side. In a loud voice I cried out, "Glory be to God! He is with us! I now rejoice. My prayers are answered fully, and my labours crowned!"

The fight, at one time was so desperate with our battalion, that files upon files were carried out to the rear from the carnage, and the line was held up by the sergeant's pikes, placed against the rear: not for want of courage on the men's part (for they were desperate), only for the moment our loss so unsteadied the line.

I lost of my company, killed and wounded, three officers, three sergeants, and 54 rank and file out of 97. Several of them, after their wounds were dressed, returned to the field, and fought out the battle.

The duke has greatly endeared himself to the British soldiers; more so in these actions then in all before. I ever loved and reposed confidence in him as my commander: but the example he gave us on the 18th, and again on the 26th of June, was sufficient to influence every man with that fortitude and determination—"With Wellington we will conquer, or with Wellington we will die!" He was continually on the first line, and frequently with our battalion. I have seen some of the enemy's cavalry charge within fifty yards of him. I prayed to God most earnestly for his protection; and I bless the Lord for his preservation. I hope his heart will rejoice in the fruit of his labour, giving God the glory due for his many signal victories.

But what shall I say in honour of my late lieutenant-colonel, William Miller, my great friend, my helper; a servant to the cause of Christ in the Isla de Leon, and to his latest breath? He is no more to be seen in this world: he was mortally wounded on the 16th of June, and on the 18th he breathed his last.

His study was to do good; and, as to military tactics, perhaps few excelled him.

His penetration was deep, his judgement sound, and his principles firm and good: he was very liberal, and a subscriber to many charitable institutions; and, if he had lived, he would have been so to more on his return to England. I have carried for him as much as 10*l*. At one time to a charitable institution. He said to me once (in the Isla de Leon), after performing a very great act for our religious society, "Don't think I do this merely out of respect for you, but for the cause of Christ, because I know it is good: and Sergeant W. Go on, and God be with you, and bless your labours." I am satisfied with the good effect religion has on the minds and conduct of many of the men; they give general satisfaction to their officers, to whom they belong.

As for Colonel Miller's attention to his company, none excelled. He was continually inquiring what could be done to make them more comfortable. "I do not care for the expense," he would say: "money is no object to me." On the close of a day's march, his first care was to see his men comfortable, and then he considered; and after an absence of any time, his first inquiry was concerning their health and conduct. Before the enemy he was cool and deliberate, vigilant and brave, firm and determined; and on the 16th of June, at the head of his company in very close action, cheering his men, he received a wound in his breast, which proved mortal.

I have lost my greatest friend, and my company a father; England a valuable officer, his parents a beloved son, and the church of Christ a friend; but our loss will be his eternal gain! Sergeant Clarke, who attended him, informs me that his last breath was a prayer.

On our march to Paris, we passed through a most beautiful and fruitful country, with but little opposition. At Peronne, on the 26th of June, after a long day's march, on our arrival, his grace gave the first brigade a job. Our second battalion carried the fascines, and the third battalion stormed the outworks in a most masterly manner, and the citadel surrendered immediately. Major-General Maitland commanded, and here again the duke was himself in the midst of it. It has been expressed that our beloved commander is not much exposed. I can fully contradict that assertion, for he is often first, and always in the midst: he will not permit others to do his duty. I believe Britain is his treasure, and his life he has pledged for its safety.

The Prussians fight exceedingly well. When we arrived off Paris, they shouted for joy, and the French trembled.

We had a grand review of all the British, Hanoverian, and Belgian troops, on Monday last. It was a beautiful sight. The Emperor of Russia was there, and many others of distinction, and his grace the Duke of Wellington on his right. The day the emperor arrived and saw the duke, he fell upon his neck and kissed him, and wept, in the presence of the guard.

I have a hut built, and an altar erected unto the Lord. My few brethren are well: their experience agrees in the blessed help they received in the late actions—peace with

God, and a full persuasion that He had a right to dispose of them as seemed good unto Him. Now they are preserved, they agree to live to and for God.

LEONAUR

ALSO FROM LEONAUR
AVAILABLE IN SOFTCOVER OR HARDCOVER WITH DUST JACKET

THE 2ND MAORI WAR: 1860-1861 *by Robert Carey*—The Second Maori War, or First Taranaki War, one more bloody instalment of the conflicts between European settlers and the indigenous Maori people.

A JOURNAL OF THE SECOND SIKH WAR *by Daniel A. Sandford*—The Experiences of an Ensign of the 2nd Bengal European Regiment During the Campaign in the Punjab, India, 1848-49.

THE LIGHT INFANTRY OFFICER *by John H. Cooke*—The Experiences of an Officer of the 43rd Light Infantry in America During the War of 1812.

BUSHVELDT CARBINEERS *by George Witton*—The War Against the Boers in South Africa and the 'Breaker' Morant Incident.

LAKE'S CAMPAIGNS IN INDIA *by Hugh Pearse*—The Second Anglo Maratha War, 1803-1807.

BRITAIN IN AFGHANISTAN 1: THE FIRST AFGHAN WAR 1839-42 *by Archibald Forbes*—From invasion to destruction-a British military disaster.

BRITAIN IN AFGHANISTAN 2: THE SECOND AFGHAN WAR 1878-80 *by Archibald Forbes*—This is the history of the Second Afghan War-another episode of British military history typified by savagery, massacre, siege and battles.

UP AMONG THE PANDIES *by Vivian Dering Majendie*—Experiences of a British Officer on Campaign During the Indian Mutiny, 1857-1858.

MUTINY: 1857 *by James Humphries*—Authentic Voices from the Indian Mutiny-First Hand Accounts of Battles, Sieges and Personal Hardships.

BLOW THE BUGLE, DRAW THE SWORD *by W. H. G. Kingston*—The Wars, Campaigns, Regiments and Soldiers of the British & Indian Armies During the Victorian Era, 1839-1898.

WAR BEYOND THE DRAGON PAGODA *by Major J. J. Snodgrass*—A Personal Narrative of the First Anglo-Burmese War 1824 - 1826.

THE HERO OF ALIWAL *by James Humphries*—The Campaigns of Sir Harry Smith in India, 1843-1846, During the Gwalior War & the First Sikh War.

ALL FOR A SHILLING A DAY *by Donald F. Featherstone*—The story of H.M. 16th, the Queen's Lancers During the first Sikh War 1845-1846.

LEONAUR

ALSO FROM LEONAUR
AVAILABLE IN SOFTCOVER OR HARDCOVER WITH DUST JACKET

OFFICERS & GENTLEMEN *by Peter Hawker & William Graham*—Two Accounts of British Officers During the Peninsula War: Officer of Light Dragoons by Peter Hawker & Campaign in Portugal and Spain by William Graham .

THE WALCHEREN EXPEDITION *by Anonymous*—The Experiences of a British Officer of the 81st Regt. During the Campaign in the Low Countries of 1809.

LADIES OF WATERLOO *by Charlotte A. Eaton, Magdalene de Lancey & Juana Smith*—The Experiences of Three Women During the Campaign of 1815: Waterloo Days by Charlotte A. Eaton, A Week at Waterloo by Magdalene de Lancey & Juana's Story by Juana Smith.

JOURNAL OF AN OFFICER IN THE KING'S GERMAN LEGION *by John Frederick Hering*—Recollections of Campaigning During the Napoleonic Wars.

JOURNAL OF AN ARMY SURGEON IN THE PENINSULAR WAR *by Charles Boutflower*—The Recollections of a British Army Medical Man on Campaign During the Napoleonic Wars.

ON CAMPAIGN WITH MOORE AND WELLINGTON *by Anthony Hamilton*— The Experiences of a Soldier of the 43rd Regiment During the Peninsular War.

THE ROAD TO AUSTERLITZ *by R. G. Burton*—Napoleon's Campaign of 1805.

SOLDIERS OF NAPOLEON *by A. J. Doisy De Villargennes & Arthur Chuquet*—The Experiences of the Men of the French First Empire: Under the Eagles by A. J. Doisy De Villargennes & Voices of 1812 by Arthur Chuquet .

INVASION OF FRANCE, 1814 *by F. W. O. Maycock*—The Final Battles of the Napoleonic First Empire.

LEIPZIG—A CONFLICT OF TITANS *by Frederic Shoberl*—A Personal Experience of the 'Battle of the Nations' During the Napoleonic Wars, October 14th-19th, 1813.

SLASHERS *by Charles Cadell*—The Campaigns of the 28th Regiment of Foot During the Napoleonic Wars by a Serving Officer.

BATTLE IMPERIAL *by Charles William Vane*—The Campaigns in Germany & France for the Defeat of Napoleon 1813-1814.

SWIFT & BOLD *by Gibbes Rigaud*—The 60th Rifles During the Peninsula War.

LEONAUR

ALSO FROM LEONAUR
AVAILABLE IN SOFTCOVER OR HARDCOVER WITH DUST JACKET

ADVENTURES OF A YOUNG RIFLEMAN *by Johann Christian Maempel*—The Experiences of a Saxon in the French & British Armies During the Napoleonic Wars.

THE HUSSAR *by Norbert Landsheit & G. R. Gleig*—A German Cavalryman in British Service Throughout the Napoleonic Wars.

RECOLLECTIONS OF THE PENINSULA *by Moyle Sherer*—An Officer of the 34th Regiment of Foot—'The Cumberland Gentlemen'—on Campaign Against Napoleon's French Army in Spain.

MARINE OF REVOLUTION & CONSULATE *by Moreau de Jonnès*—The Recollections of a French Soldier of the Revolutionary Wars 1791-1804.

GENTLEMEN IN RED *by John Dobbs & Robert Knowles*—Two Accounts of British Infantry Officers During the Peninsular War Recollections of an Old 52nd Man by John Dobbs An Officer of Fusiliers by Robert Knowles.

CORPORAL BROWN'S CAMPAIGNS IN THE LOW COUNTRIES *by Robert Brown*—Recollections of a Coldstream Guard in the Early Campaigns Against Revolutionary France 1793-1795.

THE 7TH (QUEENS OWN) HUSSARS: Volume 2—1793-1815 *by C. R. B. Barrett*—During the Campaigns in the Low Countries & the Peninsula and Waterloo Campaigns of the Napoleonic Wars. Volume 2: 1793-1815.

THE MARENGO CAMPAIGN 1800 *by Herbert H. Sargent*—The Victory that Completed the Austrian Defeat in Italy.

DONALDSON OF THE 94TH—SCOTS BRIGADE *by Joseph Donaldson*—The Recollections of a Soldier During the Peninsula & South of France Campaigns of the Napoleonic Wars.

A CONSCRIPT FOR EMPIRE *by Philippe as told to Johann Christian Maempel*—The Experiences of a Young German Conscript During the Napoleonic Wars.

JOURNAL OF THE CAMPAIGN OF 1815 *by Alexander Cavalié Mercer*—The Experiences of an Officer of the Royal Horse Artillery During the Waterloo Campaign.

NAPOLEON'S CAMPAIGNS IN POLAND 1806-7 *by Robert Wilson*—The campaign in Poland from the Russian side of the conflict.

LEONAUR

ALSO FROM LEONAUR
AVAILABLE IN SOFTCOVER OR HARDCOVER WITH DUST JACKET

OMPTEDA OF THE KING'S GERMAN LEGION *by Christian von Ompteda*—A Hanoverian Officer on Campaign Against Napoleon.

LIEUTENANT SIMMONS OF THE 95TH (RIFLES) *by George Simmons*—Recollections of the Peninsula, South of France & Waterloo Campaigns of the Napoleonic Wars.

A HORSEMAN FOR THE EMPEROR *by Jean Baptiste Gazzola*—A Cavalryman of Napoleon's Army on Campaign Throughout the Napoleonic Wars.

SERGEANT LAWRENCE *by William Lawrence*—With the 40th Regt. of Foot in South America, the Peninsular War & at Waterloo.

CAMPAIGNS WITH THE FIELD TRAIN *by Richard D. Henegan*—Experiences of a British Officer During the Peninsula and Waterloo Campaigns of the Napoleonic Wars.

CAVALRY SURGEON *by S. D. Broughton*—On Campaign Against Napoleon in the Peninsula & South of France During the Napoleonic Wars 1812-1814.

MEN OF THE RIFLES *by Thomas Knight, Henry Curling & Jonathan Leach*—The Reminiscences of Thomas Knight of the 95th (Rifles) by Thomas Knight, Henry Curling's Anecdotes by Henry Curling & The Field Services of the Rifle Brigade from its Formation to Waterloo by Jonathan Leach.

THE ULM CAMPAIGN 1805 *by F. N. Maude*—Napoleon and the Defeat of the Austrian Army During the 'War of the Third Coalition'.

SOLDIERING WITH THE 'DIVISION' *by Thomas Garrety*—The Military Experiences of an Infantryman of the 43rd Regiment During the Napoleonic Wars.

SERGEANT MORRIS OF THE 73RD FOOT *by Thomas Morris*—The Experiences of a British Infantryman During the Napoleonic Wars-Including Campaigns in Germany and at Waterloo.

A VOICE FROM WATERLOO *by Edward Cotton*—The Personal Experiences of a British Cavalryman Who Became a Battlefield Guide and Authority on the Campaign of 1815.

NAPOLEON AND HIS MARSHALS *by J. T. Headley*—The Men of the First Empire.

LEONAUR

ALSO FROM LEONAUR
AVAILABLE IN SOFTCOVER OR HARDCOVER WITH DUST JACKET

BUGEAUD: A PACK WITH A BATON *by Thomas Robert Bugeaud*—The Early Campaigns of a Soldier of Napoleon's Army Who Would Become a Marshal of France.

WATERLOO RECOLLECTIONS *by Frederick Llewellyn*—Rare First Hand Accounts, Letters, Reports and Retellings from the Campaign of 1815.

SERGEANT NICOL *by Daniel Nicol*—The Experiences of a Gordon Highlander During the Napoleonic Wars in Egypt, the Peninsula and France.

THE JENA CAMPAIGN: 1806 *by F. N. Maude*—The Twin Battles of Jena & Auerstadt Between Napoleon's French and the Prussian Army.

PRIVATE O'NEIL *by Charles O'Neil*—The recollections of an Irish Rogue of H. M. 28th Regt.—The Slashers—during the Peninsula & Waterloo campaigns of the Napoleonic war.

ROYAL HIGHLANDER *by James Anton*—A soldier of H.M 42nd (Royal) Highlanders during the Peninsular, South of France & Waterloo Campaigns of the Napoleonic Wars.

CAPTAIN BLAZE *by Elzéar Blaze*—Life in Napoleons Army.

LEJEUNE VOLUME 1 *by Louis-François Lejeune*—The Napoleonic Wars through the Experiences of an Officer on Berthier's Staff.

LEJEUNE VOLUME 2 *by Louis-François Lejeune*—The Napoleonic Wars through the Experiences of an Officer on Berthier's Staff.

CAPTAIN COIGNET *by Jean-Roch Coignet*—A Soldier of Napoleon's Imperial Guard from the Italian Campaign to Russia and Waterloo.

FUSILIER COOPER *by John S. Cooper*—Experiences in the 7th (Royal) Fusiliers During the Peninsular Campaign of the Napoleonic Wars and the American Campaign to New Orleans.

FIGHTING NAPOLEON'S EMPIRE *by Joseph Anderson*—The Campaigns of a British Infantryman in Italy, Egypt, the Peninsular & the West Indies During the Napoleonic Wars.

CHASSEUR BARRES *by Jean-Baptiste Barres*—The experiences of a French Infantryman of the Imperial Guard at Austerlitz, Jena, Eylau, Friedland, in the Peninsular, Lutzen, Bautzen, Zinnwald and Hanau during the Napoleonic Wars.

LEONAUR

ALSO FROM LEONAUR
AVAILABLE IN SOFTCOVER OR HARDCOVER WITH DUST JACKET

IRON TIMES WITH THE GUARDS *by An O. E. (G. P. A. Fildes)*—The Experiences of an Officer of the Coldstream Guards on the Western Front During the First World War.

THE GREAT WAR IN THE MIDDLE EAST: 1 *by W. T. Massey*—The Desert Campaigns & How Jerusalem Was Won---two classic accounts in one volume.

THE GREAT WAR IN THE MIDDLE EAST: 2 *by W. T. Massey*—Allenby's Final Triumph.

SMITH-DORRIEN *by Horace Smith-Dorrien*—Isandlwhana to the Great War.

1914 *by Sir John French*—The Early Campaigns of the Great War by the British Commander.

GRENADIER *by E. R. M. Fryer*—The Recollections of an Officer of the Grenadier Guards throughout the Great War on the Western Front.

BATTLE, CAPTURE & ESCAPE *by George Pearson*—The Experiences of a Canadian Light Infantryman During the Great War.

DIGGERS AT WAR *by R. Hugh Knyvett & G. P. Cuttriss*—"Over There" With the Australians by R. Hugh Knyvett and Over the Top With the Third Australian Division by G. P. Cuttriss. Accounts of Australians During the Great War in the Middle East, at Gallipoli and on the Western Front.

HEAVY FIGHTING BEFORE US *by George Brenton Laurie*—The Letters of an Officer of the Royal Irish Rifles on the Western Front During the Great War.

THE CAMELIERS *by Oliver Hogue*—A Classic Account of the Australians of the Imperial Camel Corps During the First World War in the Middle East.

RED DUST *by Donald Black*—A Classic Account of Australian Light Horsemen in Palestine During the First World War.

THE LEAN, BROWN MEN *by Angus Buchanan*—Experiences in East Africa During the Great War with the 25th Royal Fusiliers—the Legion of Frontiersmen.

THE NIGERIAN REGIMENT IN EAST AFRICA *by W. D. Downes*—On Campaign During the Great War 1916-1918.

THE 'DIE-HARDS' IN SIBERIA *by John Ward*—With the Middlesex Regiment Against the Bolsheviks 1918-19.